How to Raise a Dog
in the City
and in the Suburbs

BY

James R. Kinney, V.M.D.

FOR 25 YEARS
CHIEF VETERINARIAN, ELLIN PRINCE SPEYER HOSPITAL
AND
CHIEF VETERINARIAN, WESTMINSTER KENNEL CLUB SHOW

WITH

Ann Honeycutt

ILLUSTRATED BY
James Thurber

SIMON AND SCHUSTER · NEW YORK

PUBLISHED BY SIMON AND SCHUSTER
ROCKEFELLER CENTER, 630 FIFTH AVENUE
NEW YORK, NEW YORK 10020

THIRD EDITION, FIRST PRINTING

SBN 671-20206-5
DESIGNED BY EDITH FOWLER
MANUFACTURED IN THE UNITED STATES OF AMERICA
PRINTED BY MAHONY AND ROESE, N.Y.
BOUND BY H. WOLFF BOOK MFG. CO., INC., N.Y.

To Bruce Blair, V.M.D.

Contents

I   IN DEFENSE OF THE CITY DOG   13

II   FIRST YOU GET A DOG   21
The American Kennel Club service . . . pet-shop dogs
. . . what to look for and what to look out for in buying a dog . . . don't buy a grown dog . . . a male or
a female? . . . what breed of dog? . . . one or two
dogs?

III   FEEDING   42
Prepared foods.

IV   TRAINING   51
The dog's limitations . . . the owner's limitations . . .
five general rules for training . . . housebreaking . . .
heeling . . . jumping up on people . . . barking . . .
tricks. . . obedience classes.

V   GROOMING   70
Fancy grooming . . . plain grooming . . . groom the
dog on a table . . . plucking and clipping . . . pedicuring . . . how to remove chewing gum or tar from
the feet . . . ear cleaning . . . bathing . . . dry cleaning.

VI   THE DOG ON THE STREET   80
      Street manners . . . escalators and elevator doors . . .
      wardrobe . . . dognaping and tattooing.

VII   LOVE LIFE OF THE CITY DOG   91
      Castration . . . celibacy without castration . . . ster-
      ilization of the bitch . . . the pill . . . breeding . . .
      mating . . . pregnancy . . . whelping . . . care of
      puppies . . . false pregnancy . . . menstruation.

VIII SKIN TROUBLES   104
      Fleas . . . the flea collar . . . lice . . . ticks . . . dan-
      druff . . . eczema—moist and dry . . . ringworm . . .
      mange.

IX   WORMS   112
      Roundworms . . . how to worm a puppy at home
      . . . other types of worms . . . tapeworms . . . whip-
      worms . . . hookworms . . . filariae . . . coccidiosis
      . . . garlic.

X   FITS   119
      Types of fits . . . care of the dog during a fit . . .
      care of the dog after a fit . . . if your dog has a fit on
      the street . . . heat hysteria and heat prostration.

XI   DISTEMPER   123
      Prevention . . . first symptoms . . . treatment . . .
      general nursing . . . food . . . keeping the dog's
      spirits up . . . aftereffects of distemper.

XII   OTHER COMMON AILMENTS   134
      Infectious hepatitis . . . leptospirosis . . . meningitis
      . . . blue eye . . . inflamed Harder's gland . . . in-
      verted eyelids . . . sties . . . cataracts . . . conjunc-
      tivitis . . . ear troubles . . . ear mites . . . vomiting
      . . . diarrhea . . . constipation . . . asthma . . . teeth-
      ing . . . retention of urine . . . bladder stones . . .
      anal abscesses . . . prolapsed rectum . . . screw-tail

irritations . . . hip dysplasia . . . rickets . . . paralysis . . . halitosis . . . dental fistula . . . diseases of the reproductive organs . . . cancer . . . tuberculosis.

XIII ACCIDENTS IN THE CITY HOUSEHOLD   150
Foreign objects in the stomach . . . first-aid treatment for removing foreign objects from the stomach . . . first-aid treatment for removing foreign objects from the mouth or throat . . . electric shocks . . . falls . . . cuts . . . paint poisoning . . . arsenic poisoning . . . strychnine . . . injured tail . . . sleeping pills and tranquilizers . . . bathroom accidents . . . cigarette burns.

XIV THE CITY DOG ON VACATION   158
Bee or hornet stings . . . ticks . . . chiggers . . . porcupine quills . . . snake bites . . . sand and salt-water troubles . . . drowning . . . pregnancy . . . fishhooks . . . heat prostration . . . hysteria from thunderstorms or from Fourth of July celebrations . . . gunshot . . . garbage . . . how to stop a dogfight . . . rabies . . . method of transmission . . . symptoms of the disease . . . treatment for rabies bites . . . preventive inoculations . . . travel problems.

XV MENUS   171
Diets for toy breeds . . . diets for small breeds . . . diets for large breeds . . . diets for very large breeds.

INDEX   181

List of Illustrations

The man was a pushover.   14

He goes with his owner into bars.   17

Your child brings home a scraggly puppy from an ash heap.   22

Secretly they are always comparing you unfavorably with their former master.   28

It is conceded that females make more intelligent mothers than males.   29

She would show him the way to the safe.   37

At the end of six weeks she tells them to get out and stay out.   39

You need the strength and endurance of a wrestler.   40

A litter of perfectly healthy puppies raised on fried pancakes.   43

He'll go around telling the neighbors you're starving him to death.   45

A dog doesn't necessarily love the person who feeds him.   53

Show him what you want him to do and he'll do it.   55

He lies down on the sidewalk when you're trying to make him heel.   57

Some dogs actually cry.   61

LIST OF ILLUSTRATIONS

If the owner jumps every time he hears the doorbell ring, the dog will show nervousness too.   67

For some reason, dogs are better behaved on a table.   73

An abandoned, expectant position which the masseur tried to ignore.   78

Dogs should not make passes at pedestrians.   82

Courtships and even marriages have sprung from just such sidewalk encounters.   85

Dogs are getting dressier by the minute.   87

The dog's attitude toward love remains today exactly the same as it was in 8000 B.C.   92

There are, I am told, a few dog psychiatrists around.   94

Owners have too often fixed up fancy quarters for a prospective mother only to find that she preferred the hall closet.   100

If life in any household with any puppy can ever be called a rut.   115

Always have a dog examined after a fit.   121

Move his dish to another part of the house.   129

Hand feeding is one of the commonest solutions.   130

Dogs suffer from depression.   131

The dog will be calmer at home.   132

They seem to think they look silly in them.   157

Thunderstorms have driven more than one dog into hysterics.   162

CHAPTER ONE

In Defense of the City Dog

"I LOVE DOGS but I wouldn't be cruel enough to keep one in the city" is a criticism often leveled at city dog owners. Another is that old battle cry of the anti-dog leaguers: "Dogs should not be allowed in cities because they are disease menaces." Both criticisms are ridiculous.

It was about eight thousand years ago (give or take a millennium or two) that dog and man first started going together. They started out as business partners. They hunted together. Just why it was that Paleolithic man happened to choose the dog and not some other animal as a hunting companion has never been adequately explained to me. There were dozens of animals around at the time who could have qualified for the job; the only talents needed were keenness of scent, agility and a certain sense of fair play (a hunting companion had to be an animal who could be depended upon not to get tough over the spoils). Since this point has never been cleared up, I can draw only one conclusion: The man had little to do with the choice. The dog chose the man.

The dog evolved long before man, so he had ample time to watch and study the race for supremacy that went on all those thousands of years (he may have been in the race himself for a period before throwing in the towel—for reasons we may never know). When the newly evolved animal, man, suddenly reared up on his hind legs and started bossing all the other animals around, I think the dog figured that here was a species likely to go places, and if anybody was

The man was a pushover.

going places he was going right along. He still figures that way.

There is no record of that very first epochal meeting between dog and man, but anybody who has ever had any dealings with dogs could figure about how it went: The dog met the man under a tree one day. He smiled at him, bowed, licked his hand, chased sticks and laid them at his feet; he stood up on his hind legs, pawed him, admired him and then, looking at him with dark, tragic eyes, gave the distinct impression that unless the man noticed him, he would kill himself right there at his feet. The result of this whirlwind attack on the slow-witted Paleolithic goon was what the dog had cannily figured: the man was a pushover. The dog moved into the cave that night, bag and baggage, with the title Vice-President in Charge of Hunting.

From hunting he went into sheepherding, sled pulling and other lines of work, and one enterprising fellow even became, subsequently, King of Ethiopia. Sometime around 3000 or 4000 B.C. the Ethiopians had come to worship dogs as gods, and once, in what must have been a moment of devout hysteria, they lost their heads completely and crowned a dog (a city fellow) king. Grave statesmen, it has been written, used to gather round and submit important bills of state to him. If the King wagged his tail, the bill was passed. If His Majesty growled, the bill was killed.

From cave dwelling the dog moved hand in hand with man into the first pile dwellings, into the first villages, into the first cities, where he has been ever since. And with centuries of community living behind him, he misses—and needs—the so-called natural life about as much as his master misses the bow and arrow or the fur G-string.

Today only a handful of dogs ply a trade of any kind or even attempt to justify their existence on any grounds other than that of being "man's best friend." A dachshund, for instance, would think you had lost your mind if you asked him to go out and dig up a badger; a collie would yawn if you asked him to herd a sheep or two, and if you asked a bulldog to pull himself together and go out and bait a bull he would look at you with a cold eye and remind you that bullbaiting was abolished by law long before your grandfather was born. And certainly no bright dog would be a king today if the job were handed to him on a hamburger platter. All of which is okay with me. To be man's best friend is the toughest job in the world and justification enough for any dog, bird or man. As there are more than twenty-six million dogs in the United States holding such jobs, it is obvious that I am not the only one who feels that they are earning their keep just being dogs.

The major proportion of these dogs live in cities and, what is more, thrive in cities. The dog loves the city because he is with humans, and as I have already explained, he prefers the society of humans to the society of other dogs. In the city he rides with his owner in taxicabs; he goes for walks with him; he goes with him to restaurants and bars; he sleeps in the same room with him; he is allowed to sit at the table with him; he goes shopping with him; he meets his owner's friends, who make a fuss over him; he goes away week ends with him; he travels in trains and airplanes and by boat with him. (When the *Mayflower* landed at Plymouth, there were two dogs aboard—a mastiff and a spaniel.) The city dog, in short, has a full social life.

As for the city dog's physical health: I have been treating dogs for forty-odd years. Thirty-one of them were spent at the Ellin Prince Speyer Hospital in New York City, and I have been in private practice in New York for the past twelve. In these years I have treated tens of thousands of dogs from both the city and the country, and it is my long-viewed belief that city dogs lead healthier lives than country dogs. I am not the only veterinarian who holds this belief. At an annual convention of the American Veterinary Medical Association a while back, one of the most noteworthy papers read was a report on the superior health of the city dog. The

He goes with his owner into bars.

report was the result of many years of careful study, made and correlated by a large group of city and country veterinarians. Their long and careful investigation proved not only that the city dog is healthier, but that he lives from two to three years longer than his country cousin.

One of the chief reasons for the city dog's good health is

the fact that city dog owners are genuine dog lovers. They must be; otherwise, they wouldn't burden themselves with a dog—because a dog in the city is a responsibility. He must be groomed every day because, living intimately with his owner as he does, he must be kept clean. For the same sanitary reasons, he must be kept healthy. Rain or shine, he must be walked. He must be fed regularly. This means that the owner, perforce, has to plan his life more or less in accordance with his dog's needs. It means that he has to inconvenience himself. I doubt if many of us would inconvenience ourselves for a dog if we didn't love the dog. City owners must therefore love their dogs. They take excellent care of them, and the consequence is that the dog thrives under the excellent care.

As for the criticism that "dogs shouldn't be allowed in cities because they're disease menaces," it must be granted that there are several ills that the dog can transmit. Ringworm can be transmitted from dog to man. It can also be transmitted from man to man; from subway strap to man; from doorknobs; from eating utensils, towels, swimming pools, and from the simple exchange of money. Ringworm in a dog is a readily discernible affliction. It can be diagnosed at a glance and cleared up within a short time, and the human dealing with a case of it can take the proper precautions. A dirty dollar bill is not so open and aboveboard.

Certain manges and certain worms can also be transmitted from dog to man. Mange in humans takes the form of a negligible rash and disappears in a day or two. Worms are transmissible only if taken by mouth into the human body. Leptospirosis can supposedly be transmitted to man via the urine of the dog—and by the urine of the rat—but some researchers believe that the spirochete in this disease dies so quickly (almost instantly) after leaving its host that it would have to do some unbelievably tall hustling (and have incredible luck) to find another host to enter before it dies. There are arguments on both sides of this question. I can only report that in all my long years in practice I have never met a dog owner who had canine worms or leptospirosis, and I have met a sizable sampling of dog owners in all these years.

Rabies is the most serious affliction that can be counted against the dog. (I repeat that it can also be counted against other animals and against birds and fowl.) But it is not the city dog that spreads rabies. No epidemic has a chance to spread in cities, where dogs are kept segregated and on leashes and where inoculation is zealously practiced.

In a rabies outbreak a few years ago that killed many dogs throughout the country, only a handful of cases were reported in the cities, and during the past 20 years only one case has shown up on Manhattan Island and that was brought in from a foreign country. In the other cities, most of the reported cases were from outlying sections where dogs roamed as freely as they do in the country. Great Britain has wiped out rabies altogether—not by eliminating the dogs from the city streets but by enforcing restraint, inoculation and a stern quarantine for all dogs entering the country.

So let's have no more nonsense about ridding the city of its highly desirable citizens, the dogs. To rid the city of dogs is to rob thousands of lonely people of a companionship that only a person who has loved a dog can possibly understand. To say nothing of robbing thousands of dogs of the affection and attention that only city people can give them.

For the urban descendants of that first credulous cave man, then, I have written this book. It is not an academic textbook. It is a primer, purely, for the amateur city dog owner. In it I have made no attempt to write technically or even profoundly on the diseases of dogs. I have covered the field of common troubles, and I have prescribed simple home treatments for them where home treatments were advisable.

For complicated troubles I have urged the owner to seek the advice of a veterinarian. I have done this repeatedly throughout the book; so much so, in fact, that the publishers of the book have accused me of drumming up trade for my profession. I have done it because I think that in complicated cases it is the only sensible thing to do. The amateur can learn just so much out of books and no more, and the veterinarian in writing for the amateur can write just so much about his subject and no more without getting himself inextricably involved. The diseases of the genitourinary tract alone could hardly be adequately explained in anything less than six volumes and a course of illustrated lectures. Even then I doubt if the amateur could tell the difference between bladder stones and prostate-gland trouble. For these reasons, I have stuck to the rudiments of dog care.

I have based the book on questions that have been asked me most frequently over the years. I hope it will help prevent some of the tragedies and serve to point out some of the pitfalls that threaten every inexperienced dog raiser and perhaps, to some extent, contribute to the betterment and lengthening of the dog's too-brief life.

My kindest thanks are hereby extended to those who have so greatly aided me in the whelping of this book: Professor C. J. Warden of Columbia University; Dr. W. Horsley Gantt of Johns Hopkins Hospital; Mr. Henry Stoecker of Pillicoc Kennels; Dr. Charles Schroeder of the Lederle Laboratories; Arthur Frederick Jones; Walter N. Chimel and Evelyn Monte of the Gaines Dog Research Center; John A. Brownell of the American Kennel Club; my secretary and right arm for over thirty years, Lillien V. Cunniffe, and my kennelman and assistant for nearly forty years, Charles Terry.

CHAPTER TWO

First You Get a Dog

THERE are many ways of getting a dog—or of a dog's getting you. You may receive one as a present. You can adopt a stray from a dog shelter. You might win one in a television contest or off a punchboard at a Fourth of July fish fry. And you can go out and buy one. Also, as happens every day in the year, you can become a dog owner unwittingly. Dogs are old and experienced in the practice of selling themselves: they are, in fact, born that way, and by the time he is six weeks old the average puppy is already as wily and full of tricks as an Armenian rug salesman, and considerably more nonresistible. A puppy will usually show you first his round, soft and cuddly line, and if that does not sell you he will try the forlorn, hungry, orphan-in-the-snowstorm approach. If that doesn't work, he may start clowning it up for you, and if that doesn't work, he will try to persuade you that no one has ever loved or understood you in your whole life and that it is high time; he will guarantee you loyalty, love and understanding—the likes of which you have never known—and it will be for you and you alone. This demonstration generally winds up with the casually dropped (but carefully saved-up) final point and clincher that he is himself a "one-man" dog. Another trade catcher is the small bully. He is the one you see in pet-shop windows chewing an ear off a much larger dog; he is the one who is always at the top of the heap, and he is the one barking with showy ferocity at the monkeys in the adjoining cage or at the ones outside walking past. Attracted, you, of course, stop and watch him, and the next thing you know you are inside the shop, carefully explaining to the proprietor that you positively do not want to buy a dog, but could you just look at that little black-and-white number over there? You pick him up—and you have got yourself a new boarder.

Children are born abettors of dogs. Your child brings home a scraggly puppy from an ash heap somewhere. You protest and patiently explain that there isn't room in your small apartment for a dog. The child cries, the puppy cries, you relent—and in a year the dog is the size of a Shetland

Your child brings home a scraggly puppy from an ash heap.

pony. One little boy I know pleaded with his father for a dog for six months and for six months the father said no, and he was under the impression that he was finally getting his point over when the kid showed up at home one night with a little three-pound pup tied up—neck, feet and middle—with a rope the size of the Atlantic cable. Houdini could not have escaped it. "Look, papa," the boy said; "look what followed me home!" The dog stayed.

Weakened and conditioned and undermined in this manner by his own child, this same man later became the owner of a second dog all by himself and by the innocent route of merely going to bed. He was on a trip and one night checked into a motel that used in-a-door beds. He pulled down his bed and out rolled a small cocker spaniel, a little groggy from his interment but otherwise unharmed. Instead of reporting the find to the management in an honorable attempt to see if the dog belonged to anybody (or, you would think, out of sheer curiosity as to how a dog could get himself in such a fix), this long-gone dog lover ordered up a bottle of warm milk and fed the puppy. Then they both went to bed and had a good night's sleep, and the next morning he checked out of the motel with the dog in his suitcase.

The trick is to avoid getting a dog. I hope you don't, though. You will have missed too much warmth and merriment, even too much plain, everyday aliveness. Thoreau said he kept a dog "to stir up the dead air in a room." As a veteran succumber myself to almost all known methods of intentional and unintentional dog acquiring, I feel doubly competent to set down here for the innocent, uninitiated dog fancier a few do's and don'ts on the subject which I hope will be of some help to him as well as to the dog he gets.

THE AMERICAN KENNEL CLUB SERVICE

To start with the very best way to get a dog: Write to the American Kennel Club, 51 Madison Avenue, New York, New

York 10010; state which breed of dog you want and ask the organization to recommend a kennel in your vicinity. It has a national file of carefully investigated kennels—hundreds of them, scattered over most of the country. The AKC will be glad to be of service to you, as it is the guardian angel of purebred dogs and is naturally—and rightly—anxious to further the best in breeding. And the best in breeding, I want to make clear, does not mean breeding just for show points. It means breeding for health.

There is a tendency in most so-called dog experts to warn the unwary about pet shops. There are indeed some disreputable shops in many cities, but in behalf of the honest dealers —and there are some—I cannot put down pet-shop buying altogether. It is far safer certainly to get a dog from a reliable country kennel, but it is not always easy for the city buyer to get to one. It may be that he needs to buy a pet in a hurry— perhaps as a last-minute present, or as a quick solace to someone who has just lost a dog—or he may simply take an undying fancy to a dog in a pet-shop window and become convinced that there is no other dog in the world for him. Impulsive dog buying is something that will go on as long as there are vulnerable humans with money in their pockets, so I think we had better face the pet-shop business and try to make the best of it. Some shops, as I have said, are run by honest, conscientious—even noble—people, and I have seen a number of excellent dogs that have come out of pet shops.

The better shops generally smell of disinfectant and not of dog odors. They are clean, and the animals on the whole have a healthy, well-groomed look about them. The proprietors of good shops (who also have a healthy, well-groomed look about them) are usually frank with their customers. They will tell you the exact age of the dog (older dogs, runts particularly, are sometimes palmed off as puppies); what kind of stock he comes from, what kennel; what pedigree he has, if any; and if you are at all skeptical and want to bother, it is easy enough to check up on them with a long-distance telephone call to the source.

If you are buying a purebred dog, be sure you get a signed, dated bill of sale stating specifically the birth date, sex, color, breed and markings of your dog and the names and registration numbers of its parents and the breeder. The pet-shop dealer may have the proper American Kennel Club registration forms all in order or he may promise to send them along "later." Just be sure you get a detailed bill of sale before you put your money down. There is a very good booklet called "To Help You Register Your Dog with the American Kennel Club" which explains in detail the steps to be taken in registration. It is put out by the Ralston Purina Company, Checkerboard Square, St. Louis, Missouri 63102. Just write and ask for it; it is free.

In buying from any pet shop, try to collar a veterinarian and take him with you. Let him examine the dog you want to buy and also take a look around at the other dogs your dog has been associating with. If this is not feasible, I offer the following:

WHAT TO LOOK FOR AND WHAT TO
LOOK OUT FOR IN BUYING A DOG

In buying a young puppy, it is impossible to predict with any accuracy or even with a crystal ball what he will look like when he grows up. His mother and father may have been championship winners and Grandma the Miss Rheingold of her breed, but it might be just your luck to have your puppy take after old Uncle Rover, his mother's brother, who was the fright-wig of the family. Such minor disappointments do occur now and then, and it is nobody's fault but Nature's and that of the Mendelian inheritance law. If you have raised a dog from puppyhood I doubt that it will make any difference whatever to you if it turns out—and this is usually the worst that can happen—that his ears are a trifle short or his hind legs a little long or whether he sprouts a fashionable crop of feathers or not. If he comes from good stock, the chances are he will be a looker.

In buying a young puppy, it is likewise hard to tell what his health is going to be like. He may be constitutionally sturdy or delicate and only time and development will determine which. By close examination it is possible, however, to tell something about the dog's present health and his general condition at the time of purchase. There are several symptoms that the lay buyer should be able to recognize and be on the lookout for.

First of all, insist on having the dog's temperature taken in your presence, and look at the thermometer yourself. The normal temperature for a dog is 101 degrees. In dogs, as in humans, the point of normality varies slightly, but anything over 102 degrees should be regarded with suspicion. If a puppy's eyes and nose are discharging, or if he has a cough, or if he has diarrhea, and if he is running a fever, whether you are buying a dog from a pet shop, from a kennel or from your own mother, don't let anybody tell you the dog is suffering only from a slight cold. He probably has distemper.

If a dog is generally listless and dull-eyed, try not to fall for him out of pity, and don't accept the explanation that he has been playing hard and is tired out.

If a dog has patches on his coat, it may mean mange, ringworm or eczema.

If his legs are crooked and the joints enlarged, he probably has rickets.

Examine the insides of his ears. They should be pink and smooth and free of inflammation.

Look at his teeth. They should be white and the gums pink and firm. Discolored teeth in a young dog usually mean that he has formerly had some sickness, notably distemper.

Look at his abdomen. If it is abnormally distended, it may

merely indicate worms or improper feeding, or it may indicate some malformation. Watch out for hernias; they are small swellings usually protruding from the navel. Also examine the skin of the abdomen and the inside of the legs for possible rash, which may be eczema or skin distemper.

Also test a dog for deafness. Congenital deafness is fairly common and can be detected at a very early age. Stand behind the dog and snap your fingers, whistle or make some other kind of noise to attract his attention. If you fail to get a reaction after two or three efforts, the dog is probably deaf. It is not likely that he is just indifferent or bored.

Another thing. Most dealers will tell you nowadays that all their dogs have been inoculated against distemper, infectious hepatitis and leptospirosis and will show you signed certificates to that effect. If for some reason you are not overwhelmed with conviction on this point, a skeptical though safe assumption to go on is that the dog has not been inoculated. Have him inoculated again. It won't hurt him. (See DISTEMPER, INFECTIOUS HEPATITIS and LEPTOSPIROSIS for further instructions.)

DON'T BUY A GROWN DOG

In all probability a grown dog will already have become attached to someone before you, and you will find it hard, if not impossible, to win his affection. Dogs have an uncanny memory and loyalty for their first loves. They may pretend to like you, but secretly they are always comparing you unfavorably with their former master, who was (invariably) a much nobler person, with a much finer house, and a classier dresser; and the citer and critic will make it clear that he is putting up with you only until he can get back to the high circles in which he rightfully belongs. Don't buy a grown dog. He will make your life unbearable bragging about his former grandeur. He may have belonged to a hoodlum or a goon before you got him, but not to hear him tell it.

A MALE OR A FEMALE?

As with human beings, there is considerable controversy in the dog world over which sex is more intelligent. As with humans, the prevalent rumor—or propaganda—is that the female is. I have never seen any proof of this contention

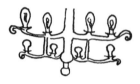

Secretly they are always comparing you unfavorably with their former master.

It is conceded that females make more intelligent mothers than males.

(among dogs, that is), and I have met—professionally and socially—thousands of samples of male and female intelligence, ranging from the Einsteins to the out-and-out dopes. Each sex has its quota of both, and I would say the score is about fifty–fifty. (The quota of "spinners"—the dog word for lunatics—is also about the same.) A number of scientific tests of intelligence have been made on dogs of both sexes— at Johns Hopkins, Cornell and Columbia universities, among other noted institutions— and their results showed the sexes close or even. These reckonings were arrived at through the application of simple but cold intelligence tests (reasoning, memory, simple adding and subtracting with the fingers and toes, first-grade spelling and penmanship, or something like that) and were not based on the biological functions of the sexes—such as the maternal. It is conceded that the female makes a more intelligent mother than the male.

You have also undoubtedly heard that females are more affectionate and more loyal than males; that males often run away but females never. This too is pure rumor. It is inherent in a dog, regardless of sex, to return affection for affection. He has been known to return so much affection for so little that he has in fact earned himself the reputation in some quarters of "selling out too easily," as contrasted with the cat, who is more demanding. If a dog has been raised from puppyhood by a kindly master, the chances are that, male or female, it could not be pried loose from that owner with a crowbar. Males and females are both prone to get flighty over sex, but after gratification (or rejection) they always come back home to brag (or sulk).

The commonest objection to buying females is their periods of heat. A number of buyers are under the impression that the bitch is almost constantly in heat, that she is unbearably unesthetic and that furthermore in heat she turns into a sex maniac. These periods occur only twice a year, they last only three or four weeks, and the evidences, both physical and temperamental, are often altogether unnoticeable. This is particularly true of the smaller breeds. As there are fifty-two weeks in a year, the slight strain of these few weeks should not deter you from buying a bitch if you want one. Bitches in the city are no trouble at all, as I will explain in more detail in the chapter LOVE LIFE OF THE CITY DOG.

Lastly, if price is a concern in buying a dog, the female, except in cases of extra-special championship lineage, is usually cheaper.

WHAT BREED OF DOG?

At the moment the poodle is still—after many years—this country's most popular breed. The German shepherd is moving up fast, however, and the beagle has moved down to third place, as is the way with vogues. The cocker held the lead for a long time, and before that the Scottish terrier was all the vogue, with his picture on Christmas cards, cigarette cases, tie clasps, cocktail napkins—and he is still doggedly advertising a black-and-white whisky. For a while there every Scotty you met fancied himself an artist's model and would strike a pose for you at the drop of a contract. Before the Scotty, the Airedale was a great favorite, and back in the early nineteen-hundreds, no fashionable dog fancier would be found dead with anything but an Albert Payson Terhune collie.

There are one hundred and fifteen breeds of dogs registered with the American Kennel Club—all sizes, shapes and colors, all tested and good breeds. There are also some fine purebreds not officially recognized by the American Kennel Club, such as—and I hope I am undermining no social careers here—the spitz, the border collie, the toy fox terrier, the soft-coated wheaten terrier and those two noble and old-line Southern breeds, the bluetick and redbone hounds. Operating out of the North as I do, I have seen not more than a couple of dozen blueticks and redbones, but they all gave me the distinct impression that they considered themselves not only in no manner wrong-side-of-the-track folks, but decidedly lucky not to have any truck with an upstart Yankee outfit like the American Kennel Club, founded only in 1884. One Georgia redbone I knew had some truck a while back with another Yankee outfit, the New York Police Department, which must have confirmed his low view of Northern customs and institutions. It was the hound's first trip to New York City—or to any city; he had never been out of his native backwoods before—and conscientious in his work (he was a coon dog by trade), he felt called upon to "tree" all the ladies he met on Fifth Avenue who were wearing fur neckpieces. He had treed them all from Forty-second Street to Radio City before the cops' net stopped him.

In the long list of dogs, there is always the mongrel—or

31

the "mixed-breed," as the sensitive like to be called. By a surprisingly large percentage of people the mongrel is still credited with being the smartest of all dogs, likewise the healthiest, the most loyal and the most heroic; there is no dog that has had as much sentimental praise or as much favorable publicity. I have seen a great many mongrels and owned a couple myself who were endowed with exceptional intelligence, health, courtesy, courage and allegiance to the home and flag, and one I recall, a bitch named Bessie—the first dog I ever owned—had all these qualities plus a singing voice. My cousin and I taught her to sing "In the Gloaming"; that is, "In the Gloaming" was the only piece my cousin could play on the piano, and Bessie would sing when he played. With the accompaniment back of her she sounded like a dog singing "In the Gloaming." Her talent went to her head, though, and she took to singing all over the place without us, and it was quite a blow to us to discover that she sounded merely like a dog howling and that it had been the accompaniment that had deluded us into believing she could really sing. Our opinion was not shared by Bessie. She kept right on singing even after the neighbors began throwing shoes at her.

The mongrel is undoubtedly an appealing animal, but he is no smarter or healthier than the purebred. Some recent and carefully compiled figures show, in fact, that he is suspiciously low in national obedience-class training. Mongrels are fast disappearing, and for their own sakes, I am glad. Their offspring are highly unpredictable, and it is they who fill up the city pens. It is heart-rending to see a pen full of homeless, often half-witted and diseased mongrels, waiting, with their tails between their legs, for a home which they will never find. If you should get one—don't let it propagate. Its offspring may be very poor specimens and their eventual owners careless and irresponsible—and either mischance will add just so many more dogs to that doomed population of strays.

As to what pure breed of dog you should buy—and it is a

question I am asked almost daily—I can only answer as I do daily that I don't know, or take your pick, or they are all good breeds. If you have not made up your mind about a breed, I suggest you go to dog shows, which are being held almost continuously all over the country, and look the different breeds over—keeping an open mind. You will see some startlingly fine breeds there that you may never have heard of because, through no fault of their own, they have never become vogues. Or if you want a vogue dog, you will see plenty of those there, of course, and at their best-of-breed. If you take a fancy to a breed at a dog show, you can find out from the handlers where their particular breed can be bought, when the next litter is expected and so on; you can, in short, do business right then and there. Or, once you have decided on a breed, you can write to the American Kennel Club as previously suggested and find out what kennels in your vicinity handle that breed. Also, local newspapers carry kennel ads, usually stating whether the kennel is registered with the American Kennel Club.

I mentioned keeping an open mind, and I should like to repeat it as a warning against some of the rumors you will hear for and against various breeds. Dog owners are notoriously biased in their opinions on breeds. Nearly all of them are one-breed fanciers. They know there exist odd-looking animals walking around on four legs claiming to be dogs, but in their hearts they never quite accept any breed but their own, and their own is usually the breed they started out with; their own is also "the only breed anyone in his right mind should ever consider," and, well-meaning and sincere, they will want to caution you against other breeds for your own good.

You have undoubtedly been told that certain breeds are vicious (chows and German shepherds are often libeled in this manner) and that certain breeds (usually the French poodle and the mongrel) are the smartest of all dogs, and you have probably heard that all terriers are nervous, that the Pomeranian is a delicate lap dog, that the Irish setter is fickle, that the boxer is a one-man dog, that all St. Bernards are wonderful with children, that any number of different breeds make the finest of watchdogs, and so on and on. The list of claims is long.

To limit myself to a few counterclaims, I would just like to state that I have known many Pomeranians who could have licked and had licked dogs twice their size (one got loose at a dog show recently and tore an ear and three spots off a Dalmatian before he was caught and disqualified for ungentlemanly conduct); I have met some dopey French poodles, chows so amiable they would hardly harm a flea, a couple of St. Bernards Clyde Beatty would not have been safe with and some Irish setters so loyal and close to their masters that they seemed like mustard plasters; and in spite of its reputation for viciousness, the German shepherd is still the favored breed trained by the Seeing Eye Institute for the Blind. I have never, in short, found any evidence that there is any such thing in long-domesticated lines as an innate "breed personality." I think it all settles down to the fact that there are good and bad, healthy and unhealthy, smart and dull individuals in all breeds, as is the case in any other species of animal including the human, and that how and by whom the dog is raised is a prime factor in personality determination. I do think, however, that breeds can be and have been harmed by too-rapid breeding, as happens in some kennels when a breed becomes highly popular and breeders are trying to keep up with a bull market. Also, too-close breeding for points, particularly where the heads have been bred for such a fashionable narrowness that there remained little space for brains, has, in the past, done definite harm.

There are two other questions about breeds that I am frequently asked. One is "What is the best kind of dog for a child?" and the other is "What breed makes the best watchdog?" I don't know the answer to either one, and furthermore, I doubt if there is an answer. I am reasonably certain, though, that all dogs, with a handful of exceptions, have an incredible tolerance for children and that nearly all dogs, regardless of size or breed, have an innate territorial instinct for guarding the property of their masters.

Children do dreadful things to dogs; they hurt them, scare them, tie them up and tease them, and the dog will take it all in a good-natured, philosophical sort of manner, or else go away somewhere and hide. Any animal is supposed to bite or react defensively if it is hurt or scared, but apparently some sort of mystical understanding exists between dogs and children beyond the conception of grown-ups. Let a grown person do only half the things to a dog that children get away with and the dog reacts one hundred per cent self-protectively. I remember once when I was a child my mother caught me teasing my dog and whipped me for it. In the middle of the whipping, the dog my mother was so nobly defending came bouncing into the room and bit her in the shin and licked my face. The fact that dogs will take a lot from children, however, is no reason why children should be allowed to tease them; they should be taught to respect a dog's feelings just as much as they would a person's; and there is always the risk that any animal, even a dog, will turn if tormented too far.

One exception to the tolerance that most dogs have for children springs from the dog's jealousy. Jealousy of a new baby in the house is not uncommon among dogs, particularly when there have been no children before and the dog has had the center of the stage all to himself. This can be dangerous. If a dog shows an animosity toward the baby and does not get over it within a week or two, he may never get over it. I know of a few unfortunate mishaps due to jealous dogs, and there is no point in taking a chance. Many dogs will take to a new baby with as much affection as its parents; but if yours doesn't, get rid of the dog. Or the baby.

There are three general rules that are pretty safe to follow in dealing with dogs and children:

35

Get the child first.

Wait until the child is old enough to know how to treat a puppy and also to hold his own with one, for the gentlest of puppies is liable to knock a small, unsteady child over just in playing with him.

Get a puppy and not a grown dog.

About watchdogs, I should say that any dog that is alert, has good hearing and can bark makes a good watchdog. In this day and age when a few quick shots from a revolver can finish off a whole pack of watchdogs, size and viciousness have little to do with the guarding of property. Some of the toy dogs are fine watchdogs because they can bark so loud. The saying "The bigger the dog, the less he barks" contains some truth. The big dog attacks and doesn't make much of a fuss about it. He figures, I imagine, that he can take care of an intruder single-handed, while a small dog calls for help. Most dogs are property-conscious and consequently are natural watchdogs.

There are a few optimistic dogs who will trust anybody. I have one at the moment, a bitch. If a burglar came into my house, she would show him the way to the safe, give him the combination, help him get the loot and offer him a cup of tea. She is young yet, however, and I still have hopes for her. All young puppies are sociable and trusting and thoroughly unreliable as guardians of property. There was a story in the New York newspapers recently about two cocker spaniels who stood looking on while burglars got into their mistress' home and removed an eight-hundred-pound safe containing $3,500 worth of jewelry and $7,000 in cash. This happened in a highly serviced Park Avenue apartment building where their alarmed barking could have brought any number of employees running. The cockers didn't open their traps, though, and after much wondering why, the reason was discovered. They had been bought off. The burglars had come armed not only with the tools of their trade but also with

She would show him the way to the safe.

several pounds of fresh hamburger, the convicting remains of which were found that night after the little sell-outs had scorned the canned food that was their usual evening meal.

To be sadly serious, I find it significant that the German shepherd has jumped to second place in popularity and that its rise began in 1963. Apart from its beauty and fine breeding, the shepherd's long-time reputation as a vicious animal undoubtedly plays a large part in its popularity in these times of crime. Doberman pinschers have a similar reputation—partly, I would guess, because they are the breed used to patrol Macy's department store at night, and their menace has been widely and accurately publicized. Several of those Dobermans were patients of mine at the Speyer Hospital and I found them invariably courteous and soft-spoken. But I was treating them, not trying to rob Macy's. I still believe it is how a dog is trained and individual temperament that make the dog—but I don't dismiss the psychological need these days for watchdogs with bad reputations.

The increasing value put upon the German shepherd as a watchdog probably accounts for a robbery I heard about recently. A woman I know bought one for her father, who is elderly and lives alone. His house was broken into about a month after the dog was installed, and the only thing stolen was the eight-month-old watchdog.

ONE OR TWO DOGS?

Some people believe it is better to get two dogs instead of one on the ground that they will keep each other company. Now and then you run across a case of brotherly love among dogs; dogs brought up together from puppyhood sometime develop an affection for each other, occasionally so genuine that they will pine away, refuse food or become seriously ill if they are separated. As a general rule, though, dogs don't give a hoot about the society of other dogs. A male dog has an affair with a bitch; then he puts on his hat, goes away, never writes and never thinks of the lady again. She doesn't even remember his name. For six weeks after her puppies are born, she looks after them, washes their faces, feeds them and brushes their hair. At the end of the six weeks she tells them to get out and stay out forever. She has a career of her own to think of; she is a companion to human beings and wants no further truck with a lot of common dogs. The puppies go their way a little resentfully at first, but after a week or two they forget all about her and wouldn't recognize her if she walked in wearing their birth certificates. In turn, they get jobs themselves as companions to human beings and don't recognize one another.

For the few dogs who are jealous of babies, there are hundreds who are jealous of one another. Most of them make this

At the end of six weeks she tells them to get out and stay out.

point good and clear, but some, like man, have learned that it is safer to go psychosomatic. I was recently called in to see an Irish terrier, for example, who was suffering from recurrent fits. I examined him for everything known to animal husbandry and could find nothing whatever wrong with him. He was in exceptionally fine condition. The trouble, it turned out, was that his mistress was taking care of a friend's dog for the summer, and the terrier could not stand the attention the boarder was getting. His fits finally became so violent that his mistress shipped the boarder off. The terrier never had so much as a twitch after that. A more forthright dog would have taken an ear off the intruder. If you are worrying about a dog's being lonely without other dogs around, forget it.

In conclusion, I have one warning to give. If you are contemplating one of the big fellows for a city pet—a great Dane, for instance, or an Irish wolfhound, or a St. Bernard or one of the larger hunting dogs—you had better have plenty of space and food, cast-iron furniture and the strength and endurance of a wrestler. These dogs eat from three to five pounds of meat a day; they can upset a coffee table or smash

You need the strength and endurance of a wrestler.

a lamp with a wag of their tail; when they are puppies and during the chewing stage, they can go through an apartment like a chain gang of goats.

Sufficient exercise, though, is the greatest problem. A brisk walk that leaves you panting is just a stroll for one of these boys. Fortunately, there are dog-walking services in most cities now where you can hire a walker by the hour, day or week, and for a fee he will trudge up and down city pavements for you after you have collapsed. But walking isn't enough. Big dogs ought to run and jump and limber themselves up all over. The only solution for large city dogs is a gymnasium, but so far there are only a few of them. Everything else has been amply provided for: beauty parlors, catering services, hospitals, cemeteries, boarding houses and schools. Perhaps it is just a matter of time before there will be a canine gymnasium every few blocks (featuring the hard workout, the rubdown, the cold shower—and the sun-tan lamp). Until then, think carefully before you take on a big one.

Now that I have cautioned you about big dogs (and I do think they are better suited to the country), I must admit that I have seen dozens of perfectly healthy big dogs live to ripe and robust old ages in cities. And as for sufficient exercise, how many country dogs take exercise all on their own? Most of them loll around on the doorstep in their shirt sleeves or sloth away their time in front of the fireplace, dreaming about walking or hunting; twitching their legs in their sleep is sometimes about the only exercise they will get for a whole day. If their owner or some other human takes a walk or goes hunting, the dog will bestir himself and put on a big show of animation, deep breathing and muscle flexing, and a swaggering attitude of "Look out, squirrel." I would hazard a guess that on the whole and thanks chiefly to the conscientiousness of their owners, city dogs get considerably more exercise than country dogs.

CHAPTER THREE

Feeding

"What constitutes proper feeding" is one of the most controversial subjects in the dog world. Wherever there are two or more owners gathered together there will be arguments. One will tell you that he has never fed his dog anything but dog biscuits and look at him—he's in perfect health. You look at him and he is indeed in the pink. Another owner, exhibiting his specimen, will boast that he was raised, man and boy, on nothing but canned meats. You look at him and he looks as fit as an Olympic discus thrower. Others will attribute the excellent health of their pets to diets of vegetables only, others to horse meat only, others to milkless and eggless or any number of other offbeat or faddish diets. A veterinarian friend of mine has a poodle patient who, for the past four months, has been given daily and staggering helpings of blackstrap molasses by an owner who claims it has cured the poodle's nervousness. The veterinarian is of the opinion that the poodle's nerves are probably quieter only because they have become glued together. He is on the losing end of the argument, though, as the owner's faith in the regimen is touching and unshakable and the dog's health so far is splendid, as is his figure. I myself have seen many healthy dogs from New

York's lower East Side who were brought up on spaghetti only, and just last summer I saw a litter of perfectly healthy six-month-old puppies who had been raised on what is as lethal a diet as any I ever heard of—fried pancakes and nothing else.

In my over forty years of treating dogs, I have found, naturally, that healthy dogs brought up on such diets, and all extreme and faddish diets, are far in the minority. In the section of this book on DIETS you will find my ideas of what daily menus should be for all sizes and breeds of dogs, from puppyhood to adulthood. Before you turn to them, though, I would like to do some preliminary explaining about them and about feeding in general:

Dogs are as individualistic as fingerprints, and their individualism shows up strongly in their feeding. Two dogs of the same size and breed—in fact, two from the same litter—will differ greatly in their food reactions. One may have difficulty

*A litter of perfectly healthy puppies
raised on fried pancakes.*

digesting vegetables, the other thrive on them; eggs or milk may agree with one and make the other sick as a dog, and so on; but any of these problems can be handled with a little common sense: just don't give a dog foods that you find make him sick.

One dog may lose weight on my prescribings and the other gain. If your dog gets too fat on my diets, though, it will probably be as a result of factors other than largesse on my part. It may be that he is the type that converts every single crumb he eats into calories. There are such demon assimilators who could wrest calories out of a meal of mattress ticking. Worms may be mistaken for overweight; they can sometimes give a dog a bloated look which appears to be fat. It may be he is not getting enough exercise or has some glandular trouble (the latter, though, is pretty rare in dogs). But the chances are nine out of ten that he is merely being overfed.

Overfeeding is the commonest error made by most owners. The normal, healthy dog, particularly the puppy, is food-crazy. He will, I can promise you, beg and plead for more food than I have advised, and you will undoubtedly give in to his pleas, as dog owners are notoriously weak in arguments with puppies over food. I want to warn you, though, that no matter how much you give in to him he will still go around telling the neighbors you are starving him to death.

If in following my menus you find that your dog is losing weight, it is possible that he needs more food. It is more likely that he needs an examination by a veterinarian. Underweight, loss of weight and an extended refusal to eat can be symptoms of any number of disturbances, some of them very serious.

I also think it might be helpful to you to have the answers to a few of the questions that are asked me most frequently on the subject of feeding in general, so here they are:

Dogs usually wolf their food down without chewing. This is perfectly natural and nothing to worry about. Their teeth are made for tearing food, and their stomachs take care of

*He'll go around telling the neighbors
you're starving him to death.*

45

the rest. This habit probably dates back to the time when dogs traveled in packs and a dog had to eat fast to get his share.

Some dogs won't eat raw meat. Such dogs are, I suppose, the truly civilized ones. Cook the meat for them slightly— enough to take away the odor of blood and the reminder of a barbaric past.

Some dogs won't eat ground meat but will eat it cubed, while others like it in big pieces so that they can tear it apart.

Raw eggs disagree with some. Try soft- or hard-boiled eggs. If they do not agree with him or if he just plain hates eggs, forget about them.

Expensive cuts of meat are not necessary. The cheaper cuts, as long as they are reasonably lean, are just as nourishing, as is horse meat, which is frozen and available nearly everywhere. Beef is the best all-around meat.

Hearts, livers, stomachs, intestines and other organic foods are also nourishing and agree with most dogs. Dogs in their wild state, I have read, used to kill an animal and, if times were particularly prosperous, eat only its insides and leave the rest of the carcass. Occasional dogs today, however, are made sick by them for some reason—maybe esthetic. I know a biochemist who believes we are a country starving to death on steaks and lamb chops and salads: that unlike most Europeans, we pass up the insides of animals, which, he insists, are the most nutritious parts.

Milk does not cause worms.

Meat does not cause viciousness.

Some dogs will not drink water. This is nothing to be concerned about. It may be they are getting all the moisture they need from their food and milk or from a source unknown to you—the toilet bowl, for instance. There is an old belief that a block of sulphur placed in the drinking water is (a) a water purifier, (b) a blood purifier, (c) a worm exterminator, (d) a tonic and I don't know what else—the list is so long. A block of sulphur is a fine dust collector and nothing else. You may have heard that puppies should not be given water at all. The reasoning back of this is that a puppy who fills up on water will not drink his milk. I would let the puppy decide this point.

There is a popular and lamentable old wives' belief that a dog should be given bones. "Save the bones for the dog," you often hear as the dishes are being cleared away. No dog should be allowed within a block of chicken bones, fish bones or any other small bones, because their sharp points may puncture the throat or digestive tract or become embedded there or cause hemorrhaging. At Speyer Hospital we performed at least twenty operations a month as the result of small-bone feeding. A large, tough bone like a beef shank, which is not easy to splinter and which has some meat on it, is a good thing for puppies to chew on; it helps their teething and it keeps them pleasantly and innocently occupied; but continued gnawing on a bone will wear the enamel off a dog's teeth. There are bone meals on the market which are good fillers and which contain certain nutritive ingredients, but there is nothing in a bone that the dog's system "needs," as many people believe to be the case.

Along with "save the bones" goes that other lamentable tradition: "save the scraps." There are table scraps that can be salvaged for the dog—a piece of prime roast beef, say, or a portion of porterhouse steak—but foods highly seasoned and oversalted for the human taste are not for the dog, and there are foods that the human digestive system can handle but that the dog's cannot.

If your dog will not eat at his regular mealtime, take his dish away and wait until his next mealtime. Don't try to tempt him an hour or so afterward.

Different breeds do not require different kinds of food. A Mexican hairless eats the same kind of food that a Scotty eats, and a Scotty eats the same as a great Dane. Only the amounts vary; the big dogs often need more filler foods— that is, foods other than meat.

47

If the smell of cod-liver oil seems offensive to your dog (or to you), try it in capsule form. If it still seems to upset him, try viosterol, giving smaller quantities of it than those prescribed in the diets for cod-liver oil. And in hot weather, give much smaller amounts of either. Cod-liver oil is usually discontinued after a year, though many breeders continue to use it throughout the dog's life.

There are those who claim that large quantities of fat added to the diet will prevent and even cure skin disorders. Fat is needed in the diet and undoubtedly has some effect on the coat and skin, but how much is hard to prescribe. In the fat line, dogs seem to like and tolerate olive oil and other vegetable oils quite well.

Two or three small meals a day are better for the dog than one big meal. And it makes life more interesting for the dog.

A dog's meal should be fairly dry. Soupy or sloppy meals are hard to digest, since the excess liquid dilutes the gastric juices and retards chemical functioning.

I have found that the following foods generally agree with dogs: beef, lamb or mutton, horse meat, fish, carrots, spinach, string beans, asparagus, boiled onions, broccoli, lettuce, celery, and fruits such as oranges, pears and apples. Also eggs, milk and cereals.

I have found that the following foods do not generally agree with dogs: pork, potatoes, fresh bread, cake, candy, cabbage, turnips, spaghetti, Brussels sprouts, cauliflower, beets, lima beans, bananas, and cheese, except cottage cheese.

And to the second list I feel I should add: cocktails, cocktail canapés and sausages, salted nuts, anchovies and all such salty and rich tidbits which people in expansive moods too often feel they must share with their dog. A small pinch of salt in a dog's food is good for him, but highly salted foods are likely to make him sick (salt is used, in fact, to induce forced nausea), as will excessively rich foods.

Of the items listed, I must admit—in a qualified way—

that alcohol is probably the least harmful. Most dogs hate alcohol; the odor of it will make them back away from it, or a sip of it will make them shudder. But there are those who will lap it up, stagger around, get sick and pass out from it. I have never known one, however, to die from it. He might think he is dying from a hangover, but who hasn't?

There are also those who develop a real taste for alcohol and, if allowed, would become sots. I know one who has to be locked up when there is drinking going on around his house because he knocks drinks out of people's hands trying to get at them. And I know another, a more circumspect fellow, who has two saucers of beer every evening with his folks —they claim it gives him an appetite—and never wants any more. They have never persuaded him to take a third drink, and if they themselves have a third or fourth, he sits and looks at them with censorious eyes. Still another dog I know goes to bars with his owner, gets loud on two drinks of beer and starts barking at everyone.

In short, occasional, moderate or controlled social drinking, while not recommended, will not seriously harm a dog. (I bring it up chiefly because many owners become alarmed when they find their dog has been drinking. Alcohol is used medicinally in many cases, as will be pointed out later on.

Vitamin and mineral tablets are helpful and, in many cases, necessary additions to diets. Almost any of the standard, known brands are good, the "all-purpose" types being best for daily use.

PREPARED FOODS

In the first edition of this book, written in 1939, I was conservative to the point of old-fogyism in my insistence upon fresh rather than prepared foods. I touted fresh meat, fresh fowl, fresh fish, fresh vegetables and fruits, fresh eggs, fresh milk; I gave short shrift to anything put up in a can or a package. In the revised edition in 1953 I loosened up to the point of giving the nod to a moderate or occasional use of prepared foods but managed at the same time to imply that the owner who fed his dog prepared foods too frequently was not a responsible owner.

I am now retreating even further. The quality and the variety and the nutritiousness of prepared foods have improved so markedly over the years that today I not only condone them but recommend them, and not only for occasional but for reasonably frequent use. Much fine research work has been done in the laboratories of such big food companies as Gaines (General Foods) and Ralston Purina. Other companies that take the quality of dog foods seriously are Quaker Oats, Swift, Wilson and Armour, to name only a few; there are so many I can't keep up with them. Even some of the big tobacco companies are now in the pet-food business. Anyhow, many dogs like these store-bought foods, the products agree with the dogs and their owners like them because they require no work. An owner doesn't even have to add water to, say, a burger to serve his dog a well-balanced meal, and that's hard to argue against.

There are also diet foods on the market for dogs suffering from heart, kidney, intestinal and other troubles. (Hill's is the brand name of one.) They too are good, but you will have to get them through your veterinarian, as they are sold only by prescription. There are also gourmet foods now for both dogs and cats. I know about them only through the ads, but if the trend builds, I wonder how long it will be before some enterprising wine company comes out with the "right" wines to accompany the various dishes.

I still believe in fresh foods, but if the menus in the section of this book on DIETS are followed for three or four days a week, I will settle for that happily—more or less. I would still prefer to have them followed fairly closely for puppies.

CHAPTER FOUR

Training

IN HIS DAY the dog has held down such responsible jobs as hunting, sled pulling and sheepherding; he has guarded property, guided the blind, acted on the stage and television and in the movies, posed in dog shows, competed in dog races, carried serum to Nome, won medals for distinguished service in World Wars I and II and tended bar in the Alps. Despite this record, the dog is still rated by most scientists as mentally inferior to the great ape, the monkey, the elephant and even the raccoon. (The dog doesn't know this.)

Fellow, the German shepherd dog who some years ago "attended Columbia University," as one paper stated at the time, probably did much to raise the dog's status in scientific circles. Fellow was the most highly educated dog of our time. He was the most publicized one, at any rate. Fellow didn't exactly attend Columbia University; he was tested there, as it was being claimed at the time that Fellow was a dog who understood the English language. Such a claim was naturally preposterous to Columbia's Department of Animal Psychology, so the professors said, "Come, come," and put Fellow through all the various disqualifying tests they had. They came out scratching their heads. Fellow understood between four and five hundred words and could execute some two hundred commands without visual signals from his master. The head scratching was not because the scientists believed for a minute that Fellow understood in the sense in which *we* understand language, but because a dog, a lowly lower-vertebrate animal, could have learned so much. Professors are very scornful of lower-vertebrate animals. They respect only monkeys and apes. Most of them will concede, however, that while the dog may not be the Phi Beta Kappa material that the monkeys and great apes are, he is the most civilized, the most cooperative and the most dependable of all animals—likewise the most charming. Such noble qualities, unhappily, have little to do with cold intelligence.

While the dog cannot be dismissed as just another dumb animal, he is—in spite of all his achievements and pretensions—still a dog, and his training must, therefore, be conducted along lines within his range of understanding. Just how wide that range is we do not know, but it is certainly wider than we have hitherto imagined. The whole marvel of Fellow's achievement was due simply to the fact that his master had been painstakingly patient and determined and had spent more time with him than any other human had ever spent on any other dog. His method of instruction was to teach Fellow step by step, carefully and patiently, to associate words with objects or activities—one word at a time, over and over and over—the dog's only guide being words of praise and pats from his master when he was right and words of disapproval when he was wrong. There were no rewards such as food, and there was never any physical punishment. In a nutshell, that is all there is to training. I have discussed training with hundreds of veteran dog fanciers and professional dog trainers, and I have found no such thing as a "method," other than praising and scolding.

The dog wants to please. His devotion to man, which has been scoffed at by skeptics on the ground that any animal will remain devoted to man as long as man feeds him, can be defended on several points. To name only one, a dog doesn't

A dog doesn't necessarily love the person who feeds him.

necessarily love the person who feeds him. Many dog owners, particularly busy city owners, leave the feeding of their
dogs entirely to their help, and the dogs go right on being
devoted to the masters who pet them and fondle them, paying no attention to the help except at mealtime. The old theory that man is the dog's God, which has also been dismissed
by the skeptics as sentimental nonsense, has been given
credence by no less august an institution than Johns Hopkins
Hospital. Experimenters in its Pavlovian Laboratories succeeded—in the interest of research—in giving a dog a nervous breakdown. It took them two months to do it, and for five
years now they have been trying to cure the dog. They have
tried everything, including sedatives, change of environ-
ment, therapeutic treatments of every kind, three months of
absolute quiet in the country and frequent mating. To date,
the only treatment to which the sick dog has responded has
been human kindness—petting, fondling, being talked to,
being hand-fed and so on. The researchers believe he will

eventually be cured by this age-old treatment alone.

The dog's memory, about which so much has been written, is phenomenal. I know a dog who remembered the sound of a motor for over three years. His owners went to Europe and left him with some friends. The friends lived in the country on top of a hill, and I was there the night the owners came back after their long absence to take the dog home. Suddenly out of a sound sleep he awakened, his ears went up, he barked, he ran around the room, he frantically tried to get us to open the door for him and finally, in his impatience, he jumped out through a window and, as the owners later reported, met them a quarter of a mile down the hill and nearly killed them with kisses. The car was an old model with a faint but distinctive old-model sound in the motor, and after all that time Rusty recognized it and knew what it meant.

The same Pavlovian experimenters at Johns Hopkins have proved that the dog can remember for a period of at least eight years, and they assume that his memory endures even longer than that; the eight-year test is simply the longest one they have conducted, and since the dogs passed this test, the researchers have no doubt that they could pass tests of much longer periods. But even eight years is a long time in comparison with human memory. Eight years for a dog is over half a lifetime. Emotionally, they can remember for a lifetime.

So the dog is highly intelligent, he wants to learn, he wants to please, and his memory is excellent. Training then should be an easy job for any dog owner. It is. Show the dog what you want him to do and he will do it. There are some minor factors to be considered, though, such as the dog's few limitations and the dog owner's many limitations.

THE DOG'S LIMITATIONS

A dog's mind tires easily. Ten minutes is a long time for even a grown dog to concentrate. So when you are trying to

Show him what you want him to do and he'll do it.

teach him tricks and his mind begins to wander after a short time, give up the lesson and go back to it later on. Several short lessons a day are more profitable than one or two long ones.

55

The dog's eyesight is his weakest sense, except in the sight-hound group: the saluki, greyhound, whippet, Afghan *et al.* Dogs of these breeds have better sight than smell. The average dog relies mainly on his sense of smell and his hearing. It is believed by most researchers that dogs are color-blind and farsighted. But a dog can see movement that the human eye would not detect. His sense of smell and his hearing are much more highly developed than the human's. A dog can hear tones, for example, that we can't hear, and his sense of smell is among the keenest of all animals.

Young puppies are difficult to teach. A puppy of less than three months is usually just so much fur and fat, and trying to teach him anything at all is like trying to teach a grass-hopper. Puppies under three months can often be house-broken, but housebreaking is more instinctive than intellectual. Dogs are naturally clean in their habits. I don't say that young puppies can't learn. They start learning from the time they are born, but their powers of retention are very gossamer during their first months.

Many professional field trainers will have nothing to do with a dog until he is fully grown. Alfred Loya, who trained dogs for the Ringling Brothers Circus for many, many years, liked his dogs to be at least two years old before he started training. And the Seeing Eye dogs who guide the blind, and who are certainly the most brilliantly trained dogs in this country, must be fourteen months old before they begin their training. These dogs are, of course, professionals, and part of the idea in waiting so long is to make sure they have all the basic qualifications—physical, mental and temperamental.

For ordinary homework such as heeling, coming when called, learning not to jump up on people and other such rudiments of good behavior, training can begin earlier, but not before the pupil outgrows some of his puppy friskiness. If you start curbing a puppy's natural play instincts too early, if you scold him for this and that and try to restrain him from the time he is born, you are quite likely to intimidate him for

He lies down on the sidewalk
when you're trying to make him heel.

life. Except for housebreaking, a young puppy should not be burdened down with a lot of restraints. If he jumps up on people or lies down flat on the sidewalk when you are trying to make him heel, he is usually just comical, and it would be a hard taskmaster indeed who would try to change him.

Leave him alone until he begins to settle down a little. Just when this is depends on the dog. Some dogs are still babies at a year or a year and a half, and some are fairly well settled down and behaving in adult fashion at six and seven months. I have seen a few dogs who knew all the answers at two and three months, but such prodigies are rare. They are the ones who grow up to be Baltos, Rin-Tin-Tins, Lassies and concert violinists.

The best thing to do for a young puppy is give him plenty of affection, which will build up his own self-confidence and his confidence in you. Then when you start bossing him around he will trust you.

Inconsistency, leniency and impatience are perhaps the chief faults to be found among dog owners. The inconsistent owner is a great trial to a dog. He will tell the dog to do something and then, before the dog has had a chance to turn around, the owner has decided that the dog should do something altogether different. He pets the dog and holds him up by his front feet one minute and the next minute scolds him for jumping up on him. He also switches words on the dog. He will teach the dog to respond to "Get your leash" and later change to "You want to take a walk?" The dog shows no inclination to take a walk or even get up because he hasn't the faintest idea what Papa is talking about.

The lenient owner is one who "hasn't the heart" to correct his dog or, if he does, gives his command in such a weak, halfhearted manner that the dog just yawns and goes on doing as he pleases. The result is that the dog eventually runs the house—a job he is not too well qualified for, in my opinion. You have to be firm with a dog. When you give a command, stick to it—even if it's a foolish one. Perhaps before the command has left your lips you have already decided that you don't really care one way or the other whether the dog carries it out or not. Give it again and make it strong. If the dog sasses you back, tell him to shut up and do as you say. Never weaken once you take a stand with a dog.

Impatient owners are probably the worst of all, because they never give a dog an even break. They haven't the patience to teach the dog anything, and they have no patience with him because he, consequently, knows nothing. It is usually the impatient owner who resorts to whipping. I know of few things in this world more futile than whipping a dog.

Nothing at all is gained. The dog doesn't learn a thing by it, and he is very liable to become cowed or cringing. Don't let anybody tell you "whipping is the only language a dog understands," or that "a dog's spirit must be broken before he will mind you." But since this paragraph is about human limitations, there will be times when, being human, you will feel your patience and long suffering snap, and if at such understandable moments of collapse you take a crack at your dog, I think you might well be excused and forgiven. An occasional bop on the backside won't harm him physically (it will only hurt his feelings), and it may well relieve the tension of the trainer so that he can go back to the tedious but more effective method of training by patience. If you must hit your dog, do it with a folded newspaper or something else that will make more noise than it will hurt. Try not to hit him with your hand. If you do this often, or even occasionally, he may begin to distrust your hand, and dogs who become hand-shy are hard to deal with.

FIVE GENERAL RULES FOR TRAINING

1. Praise a dog when he merits it and scold him when he disobeys. Praise and disapproval are the fundamentals of teaching anything, from housebreaking to ballroom dancing. Praise can be given with words, with a pat on the head, or with bites of food. The consensus among professional trainers is that food is unnecessary and that furthermore it gets the dog's mind off his work. Virtually all dumb animals will obey for the reward of food or through fear of punishment. The seal plays "My Country, 'Tis of Thee" off key for a piece of fish, and the lion jumps through hoops through fear of the whip. The monkey and the ape learn and obey not only for food, but also because they know they are the most intellectual of all animals next to man and they want to hold that status. (Some of them will even pretend to read. A monkey

59

wearing a pair of glasses is a happy monkey.) But the dog will learn for nothing more tangible in the way of reward than kind words and a pat on the head. Which could mean, of course, that the dog is a fool.

2. Stick to the same sets of words in praising and disapproving, and stick to the same tones of voice. Decide upon some word like "good," "fine," "okay" or any equivalent, and stay with it. Decide the same ("shame," "bad" or "no") for disapproval. A dog understands tone of voice better than words, and if you say "shame" to him in a sweet voice, he will misunderstand you and think you're encouraging him. Put a lot of pressure back of your words, particularly your words of disapproval. When you call him a bum, don't smile.

3. Always show a dog what you want him to do. If you want him to sit in a certain chair, for example, you don't tell him to go sit in that chair over there. You lead him over to the chair, put him in it and say "chair" to him over and over. Repeat and repeat this procedure and, after a while, start scolding the dog if he jumps off. Praise him, of course, if he stays put. After a short time he should know what "Sit in the chair" means. "Chair" will be the only word in the command he understands, but if you use a sentence, emphasize the word he understands. The use of a whole sentence merely makes him look brainier.

4. Don't try to teach your dog anything when his mind is on other important matters. There may be a cat outside the window; perhaps there are other people around—guests, maybe, who are strange to him and distracting; or there is an unusual racket going on somewhere that he feels he should personally investigate; or it's his mealtime. And, as I explained previously, don't tax your dog's mind for long periods. Give him short lessons several times a day.

5. Don't scold a dog for a mistake he has made some time before. It must be done at the time or immediately afterward. And don't call a dog to you to punish him; he will get so he won't come to you. Go after him.

HOUSEBREAKING

This should be undertaken at around three months. A few puppies can be housebroken at around two months, but very few. During the housebreaking ordeal there will be many exasperating moments when you will curse and tear your hair and call your dog's mother names. On these occasions, instead of standing up and fighting back at you like a man, he will give you that nobody-loves-me look, his ears will droop, his tail will drop—he may even cry. Some dogs do actually cry. As calculated, all this will soften you and you will decide to give him one more chance. He will promise never to do it again and the two of you will shake hands and start over. In half an hour the pail and the mop are out again.

Some dogs actually cry.

The equipment for housebreaking a puppy is simple. All you need is a voice, a quick eye, a newspaper and an agile spring to your legs. The method is equally simple. When you see the dog sit down in a squatting position, snatch him up and put him on a newspaper, which should always be kept in the same place. After you do this a hundred or two hundred times, he will probably get the idea. He might get it after ten or twenty times. The trick is to catch him just as he's getting ready to let go—which is a trick, let me tell you, because puppies are almost instantaneous. Older dogs sniff around and circle around and practically telegraph ahead for reservations. One older dog I know presses the buzzer under the dining-room table of his house and summons the cook when he wants to be taken out. If she doesn't come right away, he buzzes again. If she doesn't come within what he considers a reasonable length of time, he uses the dining-room rug. Needless to say, he has her well trained. But puppies waste no time. They're frequent, too, averaging three to four bowel movements and urinating ten or twelve times a day.

When you are too late in your snatching, which will be often, pick the puppy up immediately anyhow, scold him, and take him over to the paper. Don't scold him for a previous mistake; it must be done immediately. And whatever you do, never humiliate a dog by rubbing his nose in his stool. A self-respecting dog would be well within his rights to pull a knife on anyone who did that to him.

One holy day, and it is possible that it may be only a week or two after you've started the training, your dog will suddenly, phenomenally, of his own free will, walk right over to the middle of the paper and neatly and gracefully relieve himself there. This, I claim, is one of the prettiest sights in the world. It means that he has at last got the idea. When this happens, you must make a great fuss over him: praise him, pat him on the head, give him a few bits of food and a quarter for spending money. He will forget from time to time, but the worst is over. Continue to praise him and pet him when he uses the paper and scold him when he doesn't. He will learn very quickly from then on.

About the time your dog has learned everything about newspapers except how to read them, you will have to begin curb training, or step two in housebreaking. This usually begins at about five months. It could begin earlier, but it is inadvisable for one reason and impractical for another: you would have to go out with him at least fifteen times a day, and I can't believe that even St. Roch, the patron saint of dogs, would have the time or patience to do that. If you have a garden or balcony you might, but most city folks aren't so well equipped. They have to go up and down steps or wait for elevators which are always just four seconds too late or walk through hotel or apartment lobbies which are always just four feet too long for the dog to wait. Young puppies have such slight restraint it is about all they can do to get across the room to the newspaper. Even at five months a puppy should go out six or seven times a day; but if you are not able to take him out, he can alternate between newspapers and curbs—which is one of the advantages of newspaper training. A dog trained to the paper can always, in a pinch, fall back on the morning news.

Curb training too young is inadvisable because young puppies should not be taken on the streets. Their resistance to contagious diseases is low, and a leash or a harness is likely to disfigure them if they start straining at it too early and as often as fifteen times a day.

Curb training is much easier than newspaper training, because the sense of smell helps direct and stimulate the dog. He can tell where other dogs have been and what they were doing, and instinctively, he does the same. On your first trips out, walk the dog in the gutter or on the edge of the sidewalk and watch him carefully. If he shows an inclination to use the sidewalk, get him to the gutter fast. If he uses the middle of the sidewalk, scold him but blame yourself mainly; he should not be in the middle of the sidewalk until he has learned this lesson. In New York City there is a fine for this kind of negligence, but, more important, it is an unpardonable offense against your fellow citizens. Dog owners who permit this offense should be put in stocks in public squares and pelted.

After your dog is curb-trained, you may notice that he develops certain seeming idiosyncrasies. He will go to the same place every time, or he may have to have an automobile to get behind, or he may demand a manhole, or he may prefer the middle of the street. And very often if you change the route of your walk, you will find that, away from his familiar spots, he'll do nothing. This happens frequently when the dog is moved from one neighborhood to another. To hundreds of dogs, October 1, New York's big moving day, means constipation.

Male dogs start lifting their legs at around five months. A few start earlier. I know one swashbuckler who started before he was even weaned. Some will wait until they are about a year old.

In housebreaking always take the dog out, or remind him of the newspaper, immediately after meals and after he has been asleep.

HEELING

The Emily Posts of dogdom say a dog should walk on his owner's left side with his head in line with the owner's body. I know very little about such matters, but I do know that a dog who pulls hell-bent on a leash or a dog who zigzags back and forth across the sidewalk is a nuisance and a menace to pedestrians and should be taught to stay at the owner's side. Training for this should begin in the house, as the street offers too many distractions. Walk around the house several times a day with the dog on leash. Hold him on a short leash close to your side. When he is at your side, pat him and praise him and say "heel" or "back" to him. Then slacken the leash. When he goes ahead (and he probably will), scold him and pull him back to position. When he is back in position, praise him again. When you take him on the street, do the same thing.

The rope training method is another way that has been successfully used. Tie a rope around the dog's abdomen and run the end of it up under his collar. Use what is left over of the rope for your leash. When the dog pulls ahead, the rope will pull not only his collar but his middle. In a short time, he will figure out that pulling ahead means discomfort and walking at your side means comfort. Words of praise and disapproval should also be used.

JUMPING UP ON PEOPLE

This is a habit that most dogs have and most dog owners encourage. It is hard to be firm with a dog when he is so obviously delighted to see you; but if you want to break him of the habit, you must tighten up yourself and scold him every single time he lifts his front paws off the floor. Don't let him get away with it once. And don't let other people encourage him to do it. Scold them if they do. Stepping on the dog's hind feet just as he jumps (stepping, not stomping) is one method often used, and raising a knee just as the dog jumps so that his chest will hit your knee is another. But being firm and unrelenting with a dog will cure him as quickly as anything else.

I once asked the trainer of one of the greatest champions of all time how he would break a dog of jumping up on people. He looked at me blandly and said, "I'd tell him just not to do it." Shortly after receiving this terse answer I was in the kennel yards with him and watched him put his champ through his routine. He called his commands from across the yard in a quiet voice, and every command was executed perfectly. When he came to one, "Turn around," a carpenter started hammering on the champ's runway. At the same time three visitors arrived with a dog of their own who started barking at the carpenter, who in turn started yelling at the barker. The champ was distracted by all the confusion and did not execute the "turn around," which, under the circumstances, seemed to me most understandable. To the trainer, though, distractions were no excuse for disobedience. He was at the dog's side in a flash, in a top-sergeant voice bawled the daylights out of him and *forced* him to turn around. That is what you call being firm and unrelenting, and it was clearer to me what he meant, and how he would go about telling a dog "just not to do it."

BARKING

This is a tough one. Dogs who bark every time they hear a slight noise are nervous dogs and probably have been since birth. The time to try to nip this habit is when the dog is a puppy. If he barks at slight noises, don't scold him—try to reassure him. If he thinks he hears a noise in the kitchen, for instance, take him out to the kitchen in your arms and show him there is nothing there. (If there is something there—a burglar or something—you are on your own as to how to explain your way out.) Nervous puppies need a lot of affection and a lot of reassurance. They are also often influenced in this respect by their owners. If the owner jumps every time he hears the doorbell ring, and shows agitation over noises, the dog will show nervousness too. For the older dog, scold him and be firm about it. If he is just barking to show off, you can probably break him of it. If he is barking because he's nervous, there is little to do about it—once he's grown up.

Dogs who bark when they're left alone are problems too. To avoid this, start when the dog is young. Put him in a room by himself for short periods at first and gradually lengthen the periods. If he barks, open the door and scold him. But do

*If the owner jumps every time he hears the doorbell ring,
the dog will show nervousness too.*

it only once. If you keep going back to him, he will keep barking just to get you to come back. Instead of going back, open
the door and throw something in—something that will make
a lot of noise, such as a heavy chain. The idea is to get him
accustomed to staying by himself. An old coat with the
owner's scent on it will sometimes keep a dog reassured and
quiet. And I have known owners to leave a radio on with
good results. I also know owners who have tried everything
with no effect and have to hire dog sitters when they go out.
Tranquilizers are useful too—even necessary when the
neighbors get so fed up with the noise they start calling the
cops.

TRICKS

What tricks to teach a dog I leave up to the owner. All
that is needed is to show him what you want him to do, step

by step. I think definitely that dogs should be taught tricks because they get so much pleasure out of showing off. There is one trick, though, that always makes me cringe and that is "Beg" or "Sit up and beg." No proud, self-respecting dog should be asked to do anything so humiliating.

OBEDIENCE CLASSES

Over the years obedience classes have sprung up all over the country and are fast becoming the social centers of many communities; some, in fact, have already replaced the Saturday-night dances and the poolroom. Aside from the social and recreational advantages of these classes, or clubs, it is highly likely that a dog and his owner, joining one of them, might learn something. I am not talking about the strictly commercial training schools around the country at which you pay tuition ranging from modest amounts up to around $150, and extra for postgraduate work or special tutoring, and I mention them only because many of them function as, and are called, obedience classes. What I have in mind are the noncommercial schools—the kind, for one, that is sponsored in most cities by local civic clubs or societies and where attendance fees are negligible; in some cases the classes are free. The societies use advanced amateurs and professional trainers, and their goal is to improve the manners and social graces of all dogs regardless of breed.

Probably more widely known, and certainly more extensive in scope, are the obedience-training clubs run by local and self-governed groups, usually under the eye of the American Kennel Club. These groups charge a slightly higher, though still nominal, fee, and membership is restricted to purebred dogs. I don't say you would be thrown out or run out of town if you showed up with a mongrel—mixed-breeds, I understand, are allowed in beginners' classes in certain localities—but they are not eligible to compete in any of the classes or shows. The goal in these groups is cultural improvement plus competition in field and other trials. The classes are generally arranged in groups for the novice, the intermediate and the advanced dog; examinations are held, graduations from each grade are observed, and diplomas and prizes are given.

In well-run classes dogs get much individual attention; it is not all strictly group work. A good trainer, for instance, watches everyone, is quick to spot unconscious mistakes being made by dog owners, and will take time out to correct a particular owner, or keep him after school. And trainers are especially helpful with problem dogs. They have all sorts of trade tricks which they will pass on or share with you, and very often one will take a fancy to a dog and take him on as a private pupil. Robert Noerr, an Eastern newspaperman and trainer on the side, took on a problem dog once for special tutoring, and with the most gratifying results I have ever heard of. His pupil was bright, handsome and charming. He had all of the qualifications for a brilliant ring career, except one: he hated judges. Under Noerr's tutoring, the dog not only overcame this handicap but one year won a blue ribbon from a judge he had bitten in the same show the year before.

Dog shows are often run in conjunction with obedience-class finals, and they too are becoming increasingly popular. For a dog with really driving ambition, and with this beginning, the ultimate goal would be the Westminster Kennel Club Show at Madison Square Garden in New York and a crack at the Best-of-Breed title or—the works—Best-in-Show. Few dogs aim this high and most are satisfied—even stuck-up—with winning a local or county ribbon.

If you are interested in finding one of these groups and don't know how to go about it, write to the American Kennel Club, 51 Madison Avenue, New York, New York 10010, or to the Gaines Dog Research Center, 250 Park Avenue, New York, New York 10017, both of which have national files of groups and will tell you where to find one in your vicinity.

CHAPTER FIVE

Grooming

FANCY GROOMING

ANY COMMENTS I have on the subject of grooming must be made from the health or cleanliness angle rather than from that of the lily painter. I couldn't possibly tell you, for instance, how to trim a French poodle with all of his fancy pompons. I might make a rough guess at trimming an Airedale or a Kerry blue; they and others of their kind I know wear long drawers on their front legs, and with charts and compasses it is possible I might manage to turn out something that resembled a dog wearing long drawers on his front legs. But the fashionable and intricate cuts of eyebrows, whiskers, ears, shoulders and such take the hand of an artist, not a veterinarian.

Professional grooms are not only artists but camouflage experts. By artful retouching, they can conceal out-at-the-elbow flaws and crooked legs; they can make ears that are too small appear larger, and vice versa; they can make wide heads look narrow, chests deeper, tails shorter, hips sleeker, eyes brighter and cheeks pinker. Even plastic surgery is practiced in the dog world. It is used for lip and ear shortening and straightening, skin grafting and, of course, the long-practiced ear clipping and tail bobbing. This has been going on so long that breeds such as boxers and Dobermans, when left as nature made them, now look downright tacky, even freakish. While it is not exactly in my line, I have, in my day, fixed up a couple of harelip cases—a condition, incidentally, that will crop up for no reason in a line that has never had a case in its history. One of my harelips later won a local laurel for her great beauty. I still have her picture (autographed) and have since taken care of her children, her grandchildren and her great-grandchildren, not one of whom has ever had the slightest trace of any physical malformation. One was crazy, but a family can't have everything.

Grooming of the fancy type is found mainly among show dogs, mostly wire-haired breeds, and these breeds do not lend themselves to the sort of haircut traditionally given at home on a Saturday night with a sheet over the shoulders and an inverted bowl over the head. These dudes need professional help—at least, to begin with. If you don't know a professional groom, ask at your local dog-ware store or at the dog-ware counter in a big department store. Some stores have grooms of their own, or if not, they will probably know and recommend someone. If you bought your dog at a nearby kennel, the kennel owners will be glad to give you a lesson or two, because well-groomed dogs are good advertisements for their kennels. Handlers at dog shows are also good sources for grooming tips; as a group, owners and handlers are not only willing but eager to give advice about their breed.

After you have learned your lessons, you can buy the grooming instruments and take care of the dog yourself. Some stores give away instruction charts with the instruments, and a firm in Mystic, Connecticut, the Durham-Enders Razor Corporation, which makes excellent charts covering most of the breeds, will, if you will write telling them the breed of your dog, send you a chart for fifty cents. The fancy poodle cut is about ten dollars.

PLAIN GROOMING

Dogs who have no bench ambitions, dogs who aspire to nothing fancier than a blue-serge-suit-and-white-shirt type of career, can be taken care of at home and by non-pros. And whether show dogs or kitchen dogs, or whether they are taken to beauty parlors periodically or not, all dogs still need daily care: daily brushing and combing for the long-haired breeds; daily gloving for the short-haired. Gloving means rubbing with a mitt made for the purpose or, while harder to manipulate, a piece of flannel cloth can be used. The daily going over of the dog—and it takes only a few minutes—is, regrettably, one of the most neglected types of care in all dog raising. Most owners give the dog a bath when he gets a little too high and never touch him again until the next time he gets too high. Dogs do not perspire through their skin—only through the pads of their feet and through their mouths— which makes them on the whole much daintier animals than their owners, and in need of fewer baths. Their hair, though, does get dirty, of course, from soot and dust, but mainly from their habits of lying and rolling on the floor—just as your hair would if you stood on your head most of the day—so it is their hair, or coat, that should be cleaned every day and not their hide. And it should be done, furthermore, for health reasons. The best-kept floors are walked onto from the streets and sidewalks, and city streets and sidewalks are certainly not the most germ-free spots in the world.

The coat should also have an occasional oiling—once every ten days or two weeks—and for this you can use plain olive oil, lanolin or coconut oil. I prefer coconut oil because it is the least greasy. Rub any of them into the coat well and rub out again with a heavy, coarse towel.

GROOM THE DOG ON A TABLE

For any kind of grooming, stand the dog on a table. Dogs

For some reason, dogs are better behaved on a table.

are far better behaved on a table. The reason is probably fear of and/or respect for authority. Every day dogs come into my office and cut up all over the place until they are put on the examining table, where they will almost invariably calm right down. On a table, you can get at a dog better, and it is better strategically for the groom. A man stooping over, a man on all fours, or a man sitting cross-legged on a floor is in no position to deal authoritatively with a dog. Nobody knows this better than the dog.

73

PLUCKING AND CLIPPING

Plucking means, simply, plucking the dead hairs from the dog's coat. This used to be done entirely by hand, and there are still a few die-hards who believe that the tedious method of hand picking is better for the dog than plucking by instrument. Instruments for plucking can be bought at any dog-ware store, and instructions come along with them. A dry rubber sponge rubbed all over the dog's coat also makes a good plucker. Daily brushing, however, can be counted on to take away most dead hairs. An occasional plucking, particularly during the shedding periods, helps things along—notably the upholstery. You can get a plucking instrument that is also a stripper, which means that you can pluck the dog and give him a haircut at the same time.

Clipping I don't approve of at all. It means cutting the whole coat off close to the skin, and it is done in the summer on the theory that the dog is made more comfortable by it. It is my opinion that dogs are made generally miserable by it. Insects can get at the dog better, and the short, prickly hairs stick into him every time he moves. Also, many dogs, even in the hot summertime, catch heavy colds from their nakedness. Dogs prepare themselves for hot weather; they shed part of their coat and keep enough of it for protection against heat or sudden coolness. This would indicate that they know what they are doing.

PEDICURING

The nails should be cut from time to time, as they are liable to curl under and grow into the pads of the feet or catch on something and be pulled out by the roots. In cutting nails you must be careful not to cut into the quick. If the nail has curled under, it is safe to cut the curl off—but don't cut any farther until you have found out where the quick is. Nails and quicks vary so much in different breeds that you had

74

better ask your veterinarian to show you how much to cut off. If you should cut into the quick, apologize and put some iodine on the cut. If the cut is deep and bleeds a great deal or if a nail has been pulled out at the root, put iron chloride on it and bandage it. Many dogs hate having their nails cut. If you have one of these, let your veterinarian handle the job, as you might wind up with a bitten hand—or if not something that drastic, an estranged friendship.

HOW TO REMOVE CHEWING GUM
OR TAR FROM THE FEET

Turpentine and kerosene, which are often recommended for this purpose, are liable to burn the dog's skin. Ether is the safest and quickest remover there is. If you can't get ether, use nail-polish remover.

EAR CLEANING

Don't wash a dog's ear out with soap and water. Wipe it with cotton and peroxide, or cotton and olive oil, wrapped around your finger. Don't use sticks with cotton on them, because the dog may suddenly jerk his head and injure the ear. When dead hairs have accumulated in the ear canal, lift them out very gently with tweezers. Dogs are particularly uncooperative in all ministrations having to do with their ears or the insides of their noses. These are very sensitive zones.

BATHING

If a dog is groomed every day, as he should be, every other week is plenty often enough to bathe him, and to the dog this is being not only overfastidious but fanatic. A dog could be bathed every week, the way ladies get their hair done, but most dogs hate tub baths. It often takes two or more people to hold a sizable dog down, and the smallest of dogs will become miraculously strong and foxy at getting out of a tub, out of the bathroom and under, usually, a bed. A soapy, slippery dog under a bed pursued by a soapy, wet and determined groom is about as close to the immovable meeting the irresistible as you are likely to find in everyday life.

I don't know exactly why dogs are so averse to baths. A few reasons are the temperature of the water, soap in their eyes, and water in their ears. A dog can stand icy water—some of the retrievers even love it—but he can't stand much heat; put a dog in a tub that is comfortably warm by human standards and he will yell that he is being scalded alive. A good temperature gauge for dogs is the same as the one used for young babies—the elbow gauge. A precaution against soap in the eyes is a couple of drops of castor oil dropped into each with an eye dropper, and cotton should be put into the ears to keep out soap and water.

The first bath (which should incorporate these rules) should also be accompanied by much gentleness and much petting. I have noticed that dogs who are frightened or hurt by the first bath or two never get over being tub-shy and that dogs who have been properly initiated are subsequently more manageable.

Any mild soap is all right to use, with soap flakes or a shampoo better than a cake. Lather the dog well and rub him with two or three soapings (use a brush or a heavy cloth); and make the last rinsing long and thorough, because left-in soap is irritating to the skin. A spray should always be used for rinsing. After the bath, rub the dog with heavy towels until he is dry, and keep him in the house for at least two hours afterward. This is a precaution against colds and also a precaution against that perversity in dogs which makes them head for the nearest mud puddle right after a bath, or a coal bin or a dirt yard, where they will roll over and over and wallow around like some common razorback hog.

There is a baby shampoo on the market call "No Tears"

which some grooms use on the heads of dogs (and on the whole body) because it doesn't irritate the eyes.

Puppies should not be bathed before they are at least six months old, unless, of course, they fall into the molasses barrel or get themselves otherwise equally messed up.

DRY CLEANING

There is no substitute for daily brushing for keeping a dog clean, but there are some substitutes for the tub bath. Fuller's earth is one, and plain corn meal is another. Rub either into the coat so that every hair is covered, brush out thoroughly and then go over the surface of the coat with a cloth saturated with alcohol or bay rum. Another bath, which will not only clean but also help depopulate the dog of fleas and ticks and soothe minor skin troubles, is the derris bath. Put two ounces of derris powder with four per cent rotenone and four ounces of tincture of green soap in a gallon of water. Sponge the dog with this and rub him dry. The faint but clinging odor of this bath repels parasites for about a week afterward. Derris powder was once commonly used by the Indians for fishing. They sprinkled it on the water; the fish would rise to it and get clubbed. I pass this information along for no reason I can think of.

If gently handled, dogs will like being groomed, because they love being fondled and rubbed. I know one, in fact, who demands—and gets—a massage three times a week from a professional masseur. The first time the two met, the masseur put the dog on the bed and playfully gave him a massage while waiting for the dog's owner to get ready for his. The next time he called, the dog jumped up on the bed and lay back in an abandoned, expectant position, which the masseur tried to ignore and from which the owner could hardly budge him. When the masseur started to work on the owner, the dog became such a nuisance hopping on the bed that he was put out of the room—where he started scratching up the

*An abandoned, expectant position
which the masseur tried to ignore.*

door so badly that he was let back in; and back in, he was right back on the bed. The masseur gave him a little workout and explained to the puzzled owner what had happened before. That was over a year ago, and the dog has had his massage three times a week ever since while the owner, a harassed, hard-working, nervous wreck of a man, has waited.

In closing this chapter on grooming, I would like to say something about the current and deplorable use of deodorants on dogs. I consider them harmful if used continuously, and see no point in using them at all. I further think a continuous use of sprayed-on perfume is injurious to a dog's coat. Personally, I find the natural, doggy odor of a clean, healthy dog highly pleasing—as pleasing, in fact, as the scent of a Georgia rose. And further, in diagnosing many types of disease, the veterinarian is often helped and guided by what he smells. Maybe my main complaint is that I don't want my work interfered with.

CHAPTER SIX

The Dog on the Street

As I HAVE already said—and it can't be said too often—puppies should not be taken out on the streets before they are from five to seven months old, the age being dependent upon the constitution and development of the puppy. A small and delicate puppy has little resistance to the diseases most frequently picked up outdoors—notably distemper, leptospirosis and hepatitis—and the owner who exposes a young puppy to such dangers should be shot. I made this point overclear to one woman once and frightened her so that she bought a baby buggy and wheeled her cocker pup through the streets of New York until he was over a year old, letting him out only in the middle of Central Park, the one spot in the city she considered safe and remote from disease. The dog got ticks.

When you take your puppy out for the first time, carry him in your arms for a couple of blocks before you set him down. (If he is a St. Bernard, he should, of course, carry you.) If he seems frightened, pick him up and talk to him; and in picking up a puppy, by the way, don't pick him up by his front legs(or by his ears). Pick him up with both hands placed on his sides just back of his front legs. When you hold him, hold him upright with one hand under his bottom.

After the puppy calms down, gets his second wind, and

suggests he would like to take another whirl at sidewalk life, put him down again; and again, if he should seem frightened or begin to tire, pick him up. Don't force him on against his will to try to toughen him up, as he may become permanently frightened.

Remember, dogs have long memories. An Airedale friend of mine who was nearly a year old became so frightened by the backfiring of a truck right under his nose that he would never go on the street again. At the sight of the leash he would start such shaking and cringing that his owners finally sent him away to relatives in the country. His nerves quickly mended, and the day was set for his return to the city. He was all right driving into the city until the car hit the heavy converging traffic. His old shakes returned, and he was so generally miserable that his hosts turned around and drove back home, where he became a permanent resident. Last year—four years later—they tried bringing him into the city for a weekend. They got as far as the heavy converging traffic.

Such extreme cases are, of course, rare; but a dog's hearing is tuned up to about four times the human's and street noises are that much louder to him. As are indoor noises, such as loud radios, television and certain types of parlor singing, which have sent more than one dog howling out of the room.

Most healthy puppies, though, will love the streets, and if not taken out too early they will benefit by the air and exercise. After the first few coddled excursions, they will quickly adapt to the life there. They will scamper after every new and exciting scent, charge up strange new doorsteps and into doorways, chase after feet that pass by them, exploring everything generally and enthusiastically. This is called Headlong Youth.

STREET MANNERS

Dogs should not make passes at pedestrians. There are people in the world who do not like dogs, and as eccentric as

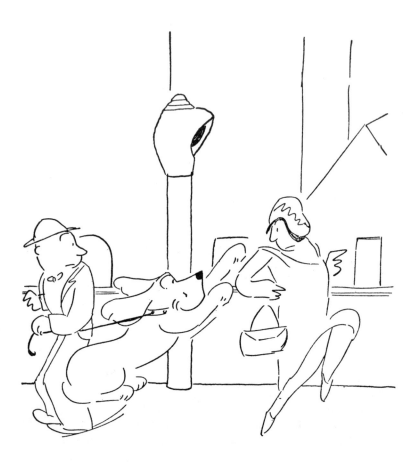

Dogs should not make passes at pedestrians.

they may seem, they have the taxpayer's right to walk along
a street unmolested by an affectionate dog.

Dogs should neither snarl at nor bite pedestrians. Biting is not only ill mannered but illegal. All cases of biting have to be reported to the board of health, and the dog is then put under observation for a period of time for rabies. If he is not rabid and if he is properly repentant, he is released on parole. If he bites again, though, he is in serious trouble. The law in New York City is three strikes within two years and you're out, and in some cities one offense is enough. The offender is taken away by the police department. If you have a dog with a generally embittered attitude toward society, one who has a chip on his shoulder or can't take a joke, time may mellow him—but meanwhile, put a muzzle on him when you take him out.

Barking at strangers on the street can often be highly embarrassing to owners. A dog will bark at a person on crutches, for instance, if it is the first time he has seen a person on crutches. To him it is something strange, and he is afraid of the strange and unfamiliar; his barking results from alarm. He may bark at a street cleaner the first time he sees one; he will bark at a woman wearing an extra-large hat, or a person carrying something unusually large or strange. I recently saw a dog barking at a man who was innocently carrying a chair on his shoulder; to the dog the man was a fiend from the outer spaces, and he was Captain Video alerting the world.

I was walking a dog myself once when we approached a couple of nuns, and inasmuch as he had never before seen a nun, he started barking at their robes. One of them stopped and began talking to the dog quietly, explaining to me that she knew he was merely afraid. Loud-Mouth calmed down immediately, and she then petted him gently. When we resumed our walk, the dog's tail was wagging and he loved nuns.

Since such demonstrations do spring from alarm and not from malice, the best way to treat them is to try to reassure the dog in a quiet voice that what is an oddity to him is not necessarily an enemy, and don't punish him except to pull him away. Dogs get used to all kinds of sights after a while, even blasé about them, but a few will cling to old animosities. One I know has never been reassured about, nor become charitable toward, horses, and he is four years old. The sight of a Central Park horse to him still almost brings on a stroke.

The use of the sidewalk as a toilet, as already stated, is unpardonable. Training for this is described under HOUSE-BREAKING.

Dogs should not sniff at or wrassle strange dogs. This is a matter of health as much as of decorum—a precaution against contagious diseases and parasites. However, if your dog shows an interest in another dog who is obviously a clean, healthy, cultured animal, and if the animal's owner does not object, there is no great risk run if the dogs frisk around a bit.

A few owners will haughtily pull their dogs away, but most of them are notoriously comradely with one another and will not only sanction the frisking but inside thirty seconds will be telling you about the time their Julie broke her leg and how brave she was through it all, and you will be telling them about the time your Johnny chewed up the razor blade and didn't get a scratch; you will swap remedies, pedigrees, anecdotes, and maybe telephone numbers. Many fine friendships, courtships, and even marriages have sprung from such sidewalk encounters. The average dog owner is not only comradely, he is trusting. The dog on your leash, particularly if he is the same breed as his own, is the equivalent of a letter of introduction with business, social and bank references and a deposit of fifty dollars in cash.

Dogs should not cross in front of people or trip them up. In especially crowded sections, hold your dog on a short leash or, if he is small, carry him, as he is liable to be stepped on. Dogs should be kept especially close in crowded stores so as not to trip up or annoy other shoppers, and they should not be allowed to chew up merchandise or get tough with the delicatessen cat.

*Courtships and even marriages have sprung
from just such sidewalk encounters.*

ESCALATORS AND ELEVATOR DOORS

Those signs which ask owners to kindly carry their dogs on escalators should say (as too few do) that dogs will positively not be allowed on escalators unless they are carried. The escalator is a perilous place for a dog. I have seen irreparable damage done to the pads and toes; I have seen pads and toes not only mangled but cut off.

Always follow your dog into an elevator—don't precede him—particularly into self-operating elevators. Those doors can close on him or, worse, they can close on his leash, leaving him dangling outside while the elevator rises. Some bad accidents have occurred in this manner.

Lastly, dogs in the city should never—and I mean *never*—be allowed off the leash. For one thing, it is against the law. Chiefly, however, dogs cannot be trusted. Unlike cats, they are impetuous and incautious animals. And their eyesight is poor. They will suddenly dash across a busy street after another dog or a cat or after some imaginary menace, paying no heed to, or not seeing, oncoming cars. Even old and sedate dogs who have never done such a thing in their lives will suddenly behave in this manner. I have seen the too-frequent and too-tragic results of allowing dogs to walk on the streets unleashed. If you value your dog, don't trust him off his leash for a minute.

WARDROBE

Available in the wardrobe line are light coats, medium-weight coats, greatcoats, single- and double-breasted coats, raincoats and sweaters; coats with pockets in them for handkerchiefs and pocketbooks for mad money. Also shoes, galoshes, baseball caps, Batman costumes, velvet harnesses, sequined collars and ear muffs, gold necklaces and, I have been told, stretch pants. I have never seen stretch pants for a dog, but I don't doubt their existence. Dogs are getting dressier

86

Dogs are getting dressier by the minute.

by the minute. It wouldn't surprise me at all to meet a dog on the street any day now wearing a top hat and a monocle and carrying a gold-handled attaché case.

Starting with the coat line, I do think it advisable to put a coat on a dog in the winter when he goes out on the street. Colds and pneumonia are common ailments among dogs, and since they never take their own coats off in the house, they get cold and may catch cold going from a steam-heated apartment or house to a cold street. Don't forget that dogs have long led the civilized life and are not as tough as they once were.

When you buy a coat or sweater, get one that covers the chest and stomach; lots of coats cover only the back and shoulders. Dogs are muscular on top and need less protection there than underneath, so whether the coat you buy has a pocket for a handkerchief in it or not, see that it covers the chest and stomach.

I also approve of galoshes. They protect the dog's feet on cold, rainy days and they protect them from the salt and chemicals used on the streets after sleet and snowstorms, which can burn. Galoshes are held on by rubber bands—and incidentally, if your dog loses a galosh, check and see if the rubber band is still on his ankle. A rubber band can easily hide under the hair, and if left on it might in time cut into the skin or interfere with circulation. I mention this small possible mishap only because I have run into it with surprising frequency during the past couple of winters, in consequence of my increased trade in galosh wearers.

The harness is generally used for small and toy dogs and the collar for medium-sized and big dogs. The choice for small dogs I leave up to the owner, but a big dog should always wear a collar for control.

Aside from utilitarian purposes, there is the "correctness" angle in the use of collars and harnesses. Regardless of size or breed, the collar and the collar only is "correct" in the high circles of the dog world, and despite the popularity of the harness, there are still any number of tradition-upholding dog fanciers who would probably faint dead away if a Mexican hairless showed up in their presence wearing a harness.

There is still another angle to the collar-vs.-harness question. Certain dogs for some perverse reason never learn to take it easy on a leash, and if they are collar wearers they may develop a chronic cough from the pressure of the collar. In spite of control and in defiance of tradition, such dogs should be switched to harnesses.

As for stretch pants, necklaces, sequined ear muffs and such, I have little to say, as they are somewhat out of my back yard, but the dog may have a great deal to say about them. I know a beautiful and vain young poodle who will not leave her house until a bow has been tied on her head, and I owned a dog once who was mortified by a plain gray coat. He had had pneumonia and I made him wear the coat when we went out. Our walks were painful. He always walked with his tail between his legs, his head lowered in shame, looking neither to right nor left, only at the sidewalk—or back at me occasionally, with reproachful eyes. Passersby also looked at me with reproachful eyes. It was obvious to them that a dog so cowed and slinky had got that way only by constant beating and by me. Danny would never have survived one walk in sequined ear muffs and neither would I.

DOGNAPING AND TATTOOING

Dognaping is still going on—but thanks to the loud screams raised a while back, the marches on Washington and the generally outraged and frenetic actions of the stirred-up citizenry, dognapers seem to have become slightly intimidated. The wide adoption of tattooing which sprang up all over the country undoubtedly acted as a further deterrent to them. Research laboratories have also been intimidated and alerted, and all of the listed ones have agreed—are eager—to return any tattooed dog they inadvertently buy to its registry.

There are a number of tattoo registries in the country now. Some use the owners' social security numbers as tattooes, some assign special numbers of their own and the best ones have national and international affiliations. I suggest you check with your local humane society or your veterinarian for a registry and for the tattooing. Many veterinarians do their own tattooing; if not, they will know where to refer you. The tattoo is done on the leg, the ear or the belly, and it hurts the dog in no way, nor does it mar his beauty, nor will he be disqualified in dog shows. Even with this precaution, it is not a good idea to tie a dog to a hydrant, a tree or a lamppost or leave him on a sidewalk or in an open or unlocked car while you go into stores for marketing.

Tattooing has long been used on race horses; it is done on the inside of the lip. It is used to discourage horsenaping and for general identification purposes, but it began as a means to identify and catch "ringers." In the old days of skulduggery in racing, ringers, as you probably know, were good and well-known race horses disguised to look like nobodies or unknowns. White feet were painted on them, or white feet were painted over with dark paint; stars were painted on their foreheads or painted out, and whole coats were painted different colors. Under different names they were then entered in a race with poor competition and, at long odds, cleaned up for their dishonorable patrons.

CHAPTER SEVEN

Love Life of the City Dog

WITH ALL his development and for all his fine civilized airs, the dog's attitude toward love remains today exactly the same as it was in 8000 B.C. He still considers love simple. He still insists that love is a matter of physical attraction and gratification, with no time lost in between, no fond, lingering notions afterward and no remorse. He has stuck to this belief, man and boy, for all these centuries.

In a world that has long since abandoned straightforwardness and simplicity in all matters pertaining to love, the dog's attitude is naturally a little upsetting. In every other way he is impeccably veneered. This worries a lot of dog owners. If the dog is as civilized as he pretends to be and as his record proves him to be, then, they figure, he has no business going around acting like some common rabbit. If he is not—if he is still just an animal—then, they figure, the unnatural life of restraint that the average city dog leads must be killing him.

For those who worry about their dog's love life, for those who merely wonder about it and for those who wish their dogs would behave more circumspectly, I offer the following advice:

CASTRATION

Castration (or "spaying" in bitches) is one answer to the problem, and a solution for people who are easily embarrassed or annoyed by dogs who are not reticent about their

*The dog's attitude toward love remains today
exactly the same as it was in 8000 B.C.*

feelings. Castration is the removal by surgery of the reproductive organs, rendering the animal sterile and totally indifferent to moonlit nights. The operation is not dangerous if done early enough, preferably at from three to ten months. In bitches it should be done before their first period of heat, which occurs at anywhere from seven to ten months, depending on their development. The operation can also be performed after the first heat, but there is always a probability of trouble if it is postponed any longer than that. For both sexes, the earlier it is done the better.

The aftereffects of castration should be considered. The dog or bitch will undoubtedly be calmer. Calmness, however, can sometimes turn into sluggishness and obesity. When the reproductive organs are removed, a certain energizing force is removed with them, and an animal robbed of that force may slow down. Other than that, the general health of the castrated animal is not necessarily affected. And today with hormones in wide and beneficial use, the slowdown can be quite satisfactorily controlled.

CELIBACY WITHOUT CASTRATION

Many dogs, males and females, live to ripe and virginal old ages without any established symptoms of distress. I say established symptoms because I have no proof that celibacy injures the health, but neither have I proof that it doesn't. I have treated celibate dogs and dogs who had been frequently mated for the same troubles, and the ratio in the long run has just about balanced. I have frequently been convinced that celibacy was the undeniable cause of certain disorders in dogs. At such times, though—and when I was surest—it invariably happened, it seemed, that immediately afterward I would get case after case of the identical disorders in dogs who had been mated regularly. I don't believe anyone would argue the point, though, that an animal should have a sex life of some kind to be normal. Since the urge is one of the stron-

There are, I am told, a few dog psychiatrists around.

gest of all urges in animals, it is sound to assume that to deny it is to go against Nature, and Nature, as we all know, can be troublesome when she is opposed. There are, I am told, a few so-called dog psychiatrists around, and in time they will undoubtedly prove that a dog has fits because his family life is thwarted and that many of the diseases and nervous disorders are directly traceable to no love.

In the meantime, granted (or not) that the present setup is bad for the dog's health, what is there to do about it for pet city dogs? The owners of bitches don't want a litter of puppies around their apartments every six months. If they do they usually want them sired by a good stud: a champion-ship stud preferably, if they expect to sell their puppies. They don't want just any dog. The owners of ordinary males will find it hard, if not impossible, to find bitches' owners who will have anything to do with their dogs because they are not championship dogs and are therefore ineligible.

The answer is that there is little, if anything, to do about the situation. Dogs will go on embarrassing squeamish people with their excitements, and bitches will go on being brazen during their twice-a-year periods of heat. Many bitches, however, remain calm and unconcerned throughout their periods. If propositioned, they will submit to a dog's love-making in an indifferent, absent-minded, while-eating-peanuts sort of way. Some bitches too, it is interesting to note, seem to have no sex appeal even in heat. I had a case just recently that was the reverse of the usual run of such cases. Most owners want to know what they can use for cupid-chasing during their bitches' periods, but this owner told me she had taken her young and beautiful Scotty for several walks in the park and not one dog had paid the slightest attention to her. She was afraid the girl's pride might be hurt if her unpopularity persisted, and wasn't there something to give her or spray on her to make her just a little less a wallflower? I didn't know of anything. Also, stud dogs in good kennels who are accustomed to such work and get high fees for their services will sometimes refuse to have any dealings with certain bitches; and a bitch very often, in turn, will fight off one of these suave, tony studs—blue ribbons and all—only to turn around and throw herself into the arms of some hoodlum dog who whistles at her on the street.

Except during their periods, bitches are not interested in love, they are not aggressive and when they are kept on leash they are consequently not apt to be impregnated. The un-spayed bitch may be an esthetic problem, but this can be taken care of as explained under MENSTRUATION.

As for the dog, there is still an old belief that mixing a little saltpeter into his food will make him sexually indifferent. I have never seen this proved. If a dog seems overly excitable, and for most of the time, have him examined. There may be a growth or malformation of some kind which is causing all the trouble. Or he may have a condition that can be relieved by hormone injections. If such is not the case and the dog is continuously upset and injures himself in his frenzy, castration should be resorted to. Comparatively few dogs have any such extreme troubles, however. Many of them will take an occasional fancy to a sofa cushion perhaps, to another male dog or to somebody's shin bone (usually some staid visitor's), or he will be relieved in erotic dreaming. Try to be broad-minded about such matters. If he becomes too offensive, try to distract him, but don't punish him. Try to remember that without these releases he might go crazy or become a criminal or something.

On the whole it is probably just as well to take the attitude that they are only dogs after all, and their love life is of little consequence, and I repeat that I have known hundreds of celibate dogs who lived to ripe and healthy old ages. If you feel that it *is* of consequence, I offer the following alternatives:

STERILIZATION OF THE BITCH

Instead of spaying, a sterilization operation can be performed on a bitch in which her ovarian tubes are tied off. This makes her sterile but still interested. During her periods, which will not be affected, she will still be hospitable but will not become pregnant. In this manner you can have two dogs who can marry and live happily ever after or, with other dog-owner friends, you can work out some community plan, the details of which I leave to you. And the responsibility.

I have heard, but I have no proof one way or the other, that dogs and bitches both, but chiefly dogs, are not as docile after mating and therefore not as good pets as they were before. I think this is highly problematical, but it is conceivable that they may be more restless after they know what it is all about.

THE PILL

An approximation of The Pill has come and gone in the dog world. It didn't work out and was taken off the market for further research. There are injections, though, that will prevent the menstrual periods from occurring; provided they are repeated, I have known them to be effective for several years. Without the menstrual periods, there is, of course, no danger of pregnancy. This method is something for you to talk with your veterinarian about in the privacy of his confessional booth.

BREEDING

Dog breeding is a highly scientific matter nowadays, just as are horse and cattle breeding. Certain combinations should be avoided, certain bloodlines crossed, certain combinations kept within the same bloodlines; when to bring in outside lines and when to continue the same lines are highly important points in breeding for health, intelligence and beauty. Thanks to intelligent breeding, many physical ailments, weaknesses and malformations have been bred right out of existence. Since it is a scientific matter, I think breeding should be left to the kennel experts who know their business. It is quite probable, however, that there are people who don't agree with this stand. Too, there may be people who want to breed their dogs for valid and good reasons that are none of my business, so I will tell you what I know on the subject.

It is quite possible, first of all, that the bitch herself might have something to say on the matter. Some bitches have a supernatural talent for getting away from their owners and getting themselves into trouble, no matter how closely they are watched. There is little in the home-treatment line to do for them once they are pregnant. Douching, even if done immediately after mating, seldom helps, and probings to induce abortion are extremely dangerous. Injections of diethylstilbestrol (of the hormone group) have been used and with effective results, but they should be prescribed and given by a veterinarian. Only if this is not possible do I suggest that you try the following treatment: For small breeds, get one-milligram tablets from your druggist and give a tablet three times a day for two weeks after mating; medium-large and large breeds can take higher-strength doses. Then sit back and wait. If at the end of sixty days the bitch gives birth to a litter of puppies, you can be reasonably certain that the diethylstilbestrol did not work.

There is a popular rumor that a bitch who bears a litter of mongrel or crossbred puppies is ruined for all future breeding purposes. This is nonsense. Nor is there anything to the rumor that a small bitch impregnated by a large stud will give birth to large puppies and be torn or ruined forever in the whelping, or else be unable to whelp them at all on account of their size.

MATING

This should be done, preferably, in the period from the ninth to the thirteenth day of menstruation. If you have your bitch bred at a kennel, to a professional stud, two services are customary to ensure impregnation. The fee for this ranges all the way from about seventy-five dollars to the hundreds and even thousands if the stud is of extra-high championship caliber. If the sire is a nonprofessional—a friend's dog, for instance—it is customary for the owner of the sire to get as his fee first choice of the puppies when they arrive.

Mating may last anywhere from ten to forty minutes, but usually takes about ten or fifteen minutes. If it lasts longer, don't become alarmed and feel that something has gone wrong. Don't try to separate the dogs whatever you do. You are liable to injure them. If the bitch becomes restless, stroke her gently and try to calm her down. Otherwise she may injure the dog. For uninterested or hostile maters a little whisky in water has been known to induce harmony, even rapport.

PREGNANCY

The period of gestation lasts as a rule from sixty to sixty-three days. The first symptom, a swelling of the abdomen, occurs usually around the fifth or sixth week. This is followed by a swelling of the breasts around the seventh or eighth week. Or there may be no visible change in the bitch at all until a few days before whelping time. This is generally the case when the litter is small—one or two puppies.

Feeding during pregnancy should be the same as at other times except toward the end, when more food will be needed. I have found that changes in diet tend to upset the bitch. Toward the end—during the last two or three weeks—add to the daily diet a quarter to a half teaspoonful of calcium gluconate.

Exercise during pregnancy should be the same as at other times except toward the end, when it is likely to be too tiring for the bitch to move around. Don't force her to take walks; and of course, strenuous exercise should be avoided altogether during pregnancy—running, jumping, pole vaulting and the like.

Watch out for constipation, particularly in the last few weeks. If there is a tendency toward it, mix mineral oil in the food (never castor oil, which might cause a miscarriage); and use glycerine suppositories if constipation becomes acute.

WHELPING

The first signs in the bitch will probably be restlessness, whimpering, short cries of pain and a desire to hide. Most bitches will prepare a bed for themselves ahead of time. They should be allowed to do this without any kibitzing from the owners. Owners have too often fixed up fancy quarters for their prospective mothers—baskets with ribbons and whatnot—only to find that when the whelping time came, she preferred the hall closet where all the rubbage of the house was kept. So let her pick her own place. Look at her occasionally to see if everything is going all right. The nor-

Owners have too often fixed up fancy quarters
for a prospective mother
only to find that she preferred the hall closet.

mal bitch will whelp a litter in five or six hours. Some will whelp a litter of six or seven in half an hour, and some will take twelve or fourteen hours and longer to whelp only a couple, but these are exceptional cases.

Because of civilization, I suppose, and the soft life, whelping is becoming increasingly harder for city dogs. Forceps deliveries and Caesarean operations are quite common nowadays. For this reason, when the whelping begins the layman should call for professional help. The whelping may be perfectly normal, but it may not be, and if complications arise they can often be serious. For instance, as commonly happens, a bitch will easily and naturally whelp all of her puppies except one. There is nothing the layman can safely do in this case. A veterinarian can try hypodermic injections, use a forceps or operate. Or a bitch may not be able to whelp even one of her litter. This too, obviously, would demand expert attention.

However, assuming that everything is normal, the owner's duties should be as follows: Watch the proceedings carefully but as unobtrusively as possible. Check the afterbirths. They are thin membranes, to which a gelatinous substance is attached, that cover each puppy. The mother usually licks these off and eats them, which is perfectly natural and all right. If there are no afterbirths, watch for them later on. If one or more puppies are born without them, and they are not passed within a few hours after the whelping is over, get advice. Don't try probing or douching; you'll only make matters worse. If a puppy should get part way out and seem to get stuck, and if the mother strains and strains and it doesn't move, take a clean towel and very, very gently ease the puppy out and give it to the mother to clean.

I don't like to squeal on anyone—particularly a lady—but I feel I should report that some mothers will eat their young. They will do this sometimes and not even have the grace to pretend they mistook them for afterbirths. Such mothers have never heard of the sacredness of motherhood and are, I am happy to report, rare. All mothers should be watched, however, until their attitude on the subject has been clearly established.

After the whelping is all over, clean the mother up a little with cotton and bicarbonate of soda solution. Put her on a clean bed as gently as you can, without disturbing her too much. Give her a little warm milk, but no solid food for two or three hours afterward. She will have a slight discharge, which will last a week or two.

CARE OF PUPPIES

Test each of the mother's nipples for milk. Sometimes they get clogged and need a little gentle pinching or massage. See that each puppy nurses and that the weak ones are not pushed out of the way by the strong ones.

When the puppies are three or four weeks old, begin weaning them. Give them a quarter or half a teaspoonful of scraped beef, raw, and milk formula (see MENUS). Gradually decrease nursing and gradually increase the feedings. At six weeks the puppies should be completely weaned.

If the mother has no milk at all, as sometimes happens, or if her supply is too scant, feed the puppies milk formula. Feed them by bottle. Doll bottles with rubber nipples—the kind you buy at the five-and-ten-cent store—are best. Sterilize them before you use them. Feed the puppies a bottleful of formula every two hours.

Puppies' eyes don't open for ten days to two weeks after birth.

If you don't want the puppies—if they have been sired by an undesirable father, for instance—take them away from the mother at birth. The mother will suffer no physical harm. Her breasts will clear up quickly, and she will mourn her puppies for an indecently short period. Massage her breasts twice a day with camphorated oil and gently press the milk out of them.

FALSE PREGNANCY

This imaginary ailment, which is both common and curious, usually occurs around the eighth or ninth week following the bitch's period of heat. Without ever having been mated she will, with this ailment, have nearly all the symptoms of pregnancy. Her abdomen will swell; her breasts will swell and even contain milk. She may go so far as to dreamily prepare a bed for her offspring. She may take a fancy to a toy or a shoe or some object and guard it with great maternal fierceness. These sorts of goings-on last anywhere from a few days to a couple of weeks, and usually with no bad results. If the breasts don't resume their normal size, rub them twice a day with camphorated oil, and if there is milk present press it out gently. Injections of male hormones have been used most effectively for this phenomenon, and if you have a stubborn or persistent case on your hands see your veterinarian about the treatment.

MENSTRUATION

This lasts from three to four weeks and begins around the eighth or ninth month, depending on the bitch's development. It can begin as early as the fifth or sixth month, or as late as at a year. In the summer months it often begins early. It generally recurs every six months, but some bitches have only one period a year. As they grow older, the periods become farther apart, but seldom stop altogether. In other words, a bitch could, if inclined, become pregnant right up to old age. And in males I have found sperm cells in urine tests of dogs sixteen and seventeen years old, which means that they too, if inclined, could still impregnate—and most of them are inclined.

CHAPTER EIGHT

Skin Troubles

FLEAS

FLEAS are disease carriers to a certain extent, but disease carrying is pretty much a side line with them. Their main job in this world is to annoy dogs—a job which they fulfill with a zest and efficiency unmatched in any other known insect, beast or bird. Fleas are crazy about their work.

Fortunately, in spite of their verve, fleas are not hard to get rid of. The derris powder–and–rotenone bath described under GROOMING is one combatant. Then there are various commercial preparations that come in both powder and liquid forms. Watch the dog carefully during treatment with these to see that he does not lick the stuff off. Stand him on papers when applications are being made, and burn the papers immediately afterward: the reason being that fleas are sometimes only stunned by the product—or may be only playing possum.

Other remedies—old-fashioned but still good—are the Creolin bath and the kerosene-and-milk bath. Use two or three teaspoonfuls of Creolin to a gallon of water; sponge the dog all over with it, but don't get it in his eyes; leave it on half an hour; then give him a soap-and-water bath. The Creolin odor will cling to him for two or three days afterward, and during that time he will be safe from fleas. For the kerosene bath, use a tablespoonful to a quart of milk, sponge into the coat and leave on for half an hour before bathing.

There is no permanent preventive for fleas. The too-frequent use of Creolin (or any of the insecticides) can cause skin troubles, so watch for fleas and try to catch them early. Fleas appear first, as a rule, on the inside of the thighs and on the abdomen, and a daily check there, and picking them off by hand, would prevent a lot of wear and tear later on.

This is a collar treated with a special insecticide dispensed by a special process. It is worn in addition to the dog's own collar, its powers are potent for a limited time and a new collar must be bought, and many owners have reported to me that such collars work miraculously. In some cases, they seemingly cause a rash. Some owners, too, have supposedly developed skin irritations from handling them. But the collars have been on the market so long now that I suppose nothing too dire can be the matter with them. Just watch them.

LICE

The louse is everything its name suggests. It is a disease carrier, a biter, a bloodsucker and a sneak. It is so small and drab it can hide itself in the dog's coat and defy detection, and its bite, not so forthright as the flea's, will go unnoticed at first by the dog. And there it hides, begetting other lice that in lightning turn beget others until the dog is good and lousy before either of you knows it. The louse is the fastest begetter of any known organism and you wonder that he has time for anything else.

If your dog scratches a lot and you know he has no skin

trouble or fleas, suspect lice. Examine him with a magnifying glass, since lice cannot always be seen with the naked eye. I don't think it is necessary for me to describe a louse to you. You will recognize it because it looks exactly like a louse— small, grayish, squirmy and sneaky-looking; it will be partially embedded in the skin, and its eggs will be glued to the hairs. The small, white eggs, or nits, can be more readily seen than the lice.

Insecticides and treatments for lice are the same as for fleas, with the additional job of fine-tooth combing, which is most important and the only sure way of getting the eggs out of the coat. If left in, they will quickly hatch and start begetting, and the dog will shortly be host to a whole new army of begetters. Use the finest-toothed comb the dog's coat will take (combs come in varying degrees of fineness); comb him on papers, and burn the papers immediately afterward. Also burn his bedding and give him fresh paper bedding daily until he is completely deloused.

TICKS

Once considered a country pest, ticks are now widely prevalent in cities, particularly in the summer, and they are a real mess. They are found in the parks and on the bushes and hedges in front of apartment houses; they live inside houses and inside furniture. They are said to be able to swim, fly, float and crawl, and they can apparently hibernate for years. I know several dog owners who have called in the exterminators to get ticks out of their apartments, and I know one who finally found the source, after recurrent infestations, in an antique desk he had bought at an auction.

There are all kinds of preparations on the market for ticks, and the treatments for fleas and lice already described hold for the smaller ticks, but it has been my experience that the use of anything strong enough to kill a big, strong-willed tick will injure the dog's skin or coat.

There are also pill repellents to be had which work well with some dogs. But there is no treatment to replace the daily going over by hand. Ticks don't rush the dog and cover him. Even in heavily infested areas a few at a time will climb aboard him, probably only one or two—but get them off fast. Pull them out with tweezers and either burn them quickly or drop them into kerosene or alcohol. Look your dog over daily, particularly behind the ears and between the toes.

DANDRUFF

Dandruff can be caused by too much bathing or it can be the result of uncleanliness; digestive disturbances can cause it, as can overheated living quarters; sometimes it is an indication of parasites, and often there is no assignable reason for it. If the dog is clean and free of parasites, the following treatment should clear up the drandruff: sponge him with bay rum diluted in water; then rub coconut oil into his coat and rub it out again. Do this three times a week and bathe him once a week until the condition clears up and he can again wear a blue serge suit without embarrassment. I know some owners who use their own dandruff shampoos on their dogs with good results.

ECZEMA—MOIST AND DRY

"Eczema" is a loose word that covers a broad field in skin irritations, too numerous and too complicated to go into here. Almost any skin irritation that is noncontagious is diagnosed as eczema. As is the case with dandruff, the causes are numerous: uncleanliness, overheated living quarters, overfeeding, parasites, nervousness and hormone imbalance.

Moist eczema and dry eczema are the types most commonly found. The dry form is more common that the moist. As its name suggests, dry eczema is dry and scaly. Patches appear in the dog's coat, the hair falls out and the dog aggravates and spreads the irritation by scratching and biting. Eczema of either kind spreads quickly, and the first step in treatment is to check it. If the dog scratches a lot, a Queen Elizabeth collar (as illustrated on page 157) should be put on him. For dry eczema, apply the following preparation with cotton two or three times a day: one ounce balsam of Peru, one teaspoonful Creolin and enough alcohol to make eight ounces. A druggist will mix this for you or you can buy the ingredients and mix them at home. It is a messy treatment in that it is sticky, so bathe the dog every two or three days during treatment if it will make either of you happier. He should be bathed at the end of the treatment anyhow.

Moist eczema appears in patches like dry eczema, but the patches are raw and red. The moist form looks worse than the dry form but is usually easier to clear up. For moist eczema, the following preparation should be applied with cotton to the sore spots twice a day: five per cent solution of tannic acid and salicylic acid in alcohol. It can be bought at any drugstore. After the sores have healed over and scabs have formed, five per cent boric acid ointment should be used. The hair on long-haired breeds should be clipped around the affected parts during treatment.

The solution used for moist eczema is not messy, and a bath should be given only after the treatment is discontinued.

During treatment of either dry or moist eczema, a mild laxative should be given—half a teaspoonful to a tablespoonful of milk of magnesia three times a week, depending on the size of the dog. Add vitamin A tablets to his diet, and bicarbonate of soda or calcium gluconate—a quarter teaspoonful in his food twice a day. Pyribenzamine (one of the antihistamines) has also been found to be effective in treatment of eczema. Give one 50-milligram tablet a day to a small breed —smaller doses for toys and larger for bigger breeds. Don't become alarmed if this medication makes the dog a little groggy or drowsy. Tranquilizers are widely used in many skin troubles, as so many of them have nervous origins.

With either of the eczemas, if there is no improvement after a week or ten days of the foregoing treatments, if the patches spread or if the condition recurs frequently, you had better get further advice, because eczema can be a stubborn disease. Only a veterinarian can treat it if it is caused by a hormone imbalance, if X-ray treatment is required, if vitamin or other injections are needed or, in rare cases, when castration might be called for.

RINGWORM

The ringworm sore is round, from the size of a dime to that of a half dollar, and is usually elevated and discharging pus. Plain iodine is used in treating ringworm. Paint with iodine and in a few minutes wipe it off with alcohol. Do this three or four times a day. If the sores are on the legs only, they can be bandaged. Rubber gloves should be used in treating ringworm, because it is contagious to humans. Keep the dog away from children and off beds. Severe cases of ringworm should be treated by X-ray methods.

MANGE

The two forms of mange found among dogs are sarcoptic and follicular. Since the symptoms of the two are sometimes indistinguishable in appearance even to a veterinarian, I see little point in going into any detailed description here. What the owner must be on the lookout for are the following general symptoms:

Mange (either kind) usually, but not always, appears first around the face, neck and shoulders. It can take the form of red, mean-looking pustular spots, or it can be dry and scaly. Sometimes the skin remains, to the naked eye, unaffected, but the hair falls out in spots or becomes thin. The dog may or may not scratch a lot, depending on the type of mange he has. Itching is characteristic of sarcoptic but not necessarily of follicular. (Eczemas, it must be remembered, have almost the identical symptoms. Dry eczema particularly is often mistaken for mange and vice versa.)

The best thing to do when you see any of these symptoms is to get to a veterinarian—who, if there is any doubt in his mind about the ailment, will make a scraping, which means that he will scrape a little of the skin and examine it under a microscope for mites. Sometimes this is the only possible way to make a correct diagnosis. More often, however, there are certain obvious symptoms in mange that a veterinarian can spot at a glance. Many experienced dog raisers can do the same, but this book is for beginners.

If it is not possible to get professional advice, the Creolin-and-balsam of Peru home treatment prescribed for dry eczema can be helpful for both kinds of mange. Also use the Elizabeth collar, bathe the dog after treatment and keep a vigilant eye out for new spots—because sometimes when it would seem that you have everything under control a new spot will suddenly appear, perhaps on an altogether different part of the body.

In severe cases of mange—when most of the body is covered—treat a third of the body a day: the legs and hind part one day, the middle the next and so on.

In treating mange, always wear rubber gloves. Although such transmissions are extremely rare, it can be transmitted to humans. It affects the human lightly in the form of negligible rash and quickly disappears. (Mange mites apparently care little for human hosts.) Also, burn the dog's sleeping quarters: his bedding, I mean—not the whole house.

Mange, when localized and if not too virulent in form, can often be cleared up within a few days or a week. On the other hand, I want to warn you that mange can be the stubbornest disease a dog can get. I have had any number of cases that took a year to cure. Once mange gets a good hold on a dog, it is not only annoying and unsightly, but devitalizing.

I have seen few severe cases of eczema or mange in clean dogs. In really clean dogs—dogs that are brushed and groomed every day—I have rarely seen even a mild case of either. I don't want to point or name names, but there are an awful lot of dogs who get skin troubles, or whose skin troubles become aggravated, solely because they are just plain dirty.

CHAPTER NINE

Worms

WITHOUT DOUBT, the most overworked diagnosis in all dog raising is "worms." If a dog chews his feet, he has worms. If he chases his tail, he has worms. If he gnaws at a plaster wall, if he lies on his back, if his legs twitch in his sleep, he has worms. There is almost nothing the poor dog can do or fail to do that does not evoke from somebody a quick diagnosis of worms. Also heard all around is that lamentable cure for all ills: "Worm him and he'll be all right." It doesn't matter what the trouble is; the dog may be suffering from any one of a dozen ailments; but "a good dose of worm medicine" is supposed to fix him right up. And still another loose piece of advice is: "A dog should be wormed every week until he is grown."

This sort of advice, hit-or-miss diagnosing and unwarranted dosing with worm medicines have done more harm to dogs than worms ever did. For every dog sick with worms there must be fifty unnecessarily sick from worm medicines.

The problem is a fairly simple one. Most dogs do have worms. The common run of worms is nothing to be alarmed about, and it becomes serious only when neglected or when the dog is dosed to the hilt with some patent medicine which may or may not be good. Some of the patent medicines are good. Some are made of the same ingredients your veterinarian might prescribe. Some are not. Vermifuges are particularly dangerous because most of them (if they are any good) have poisons in them which, if they are given too freely, will not only kill the worms but also cause serious harm to the dog. If they don't contain these poisons, you have wasted your time and money and made your dog sick to no avail because he will still have his worms. Furthermore, a correct dosage for one dog might be an overdose for another. So don't dose up your dog without a diagnosis—and that can be properly done only by microscopic examination of his stool and/or blood and by your veterinarian.

ROUNDWORMS

An exception to the foregoing is roundworms—or "puppy worms," as they are commonly called—which can be diagnosed and treated at home. And I strongly believe that except for emergencies, young puppies *should* be treated at home and not in hospitals or clinics: the best-run of them are not germproof, and in his early months a puppy's resistance to contagious disease is low and doubly so if he is wormy.

Roundworms are easy to diagnose, because they can be seen in the puppy's stool—or, as is frequently the case, he will vomit them up. They are nearly always curled up and are generally two or three inches long, but sometimes they come as long as ten or twelve inches. The treatment is as follows:

5 teaspoonfuls castor oil
3 teaspoonfuls syrup of buckthorn
6 drops oil of wormseed

Give a teaspoonful to toy puppies, two teaspoonfuls to small-breed puppies and a tablespoonful to large-breed puppies. The same dosage should be repeated every three or four

113

weeks or until the puppy has had three or four wormings. Later, if the worms start reappearing, repeat the treatments, increasing the dosage slightly, as he should be tougher by this time.

HOW TO WORM A PUPPY AT HOME

Contrary to the common belief that worming a puppy is a nuisance, that bowel actions go on for days and that the dog himself nearly dies from weakness, the procedure is easy and simple. Medicine is given in the morning on an empty stomach; four, five or six hours later, action will begin, and after two or three bowel movements it is all over.

A puppy should not be wormed before he is eight weeks old unless his stool and vomitus indicate that he is more worm than dog, which is rare. The bathroom is a good place to keep him on the day he is wormed. Spread papers over the entire floor, and when it is about time for things to start happening, put him in there and keep him in there until the first action. Then put fresh papers down and let the prisoner out for a few minutes before you put him back. Give him a shank bone or a knucklebone to chew on during the incarceration or he will get bored and howl. I know a woman who put a radio in the bathroom to keep her dog entertained. He was entertained highly; he chewed all the knobs off it. By late afternoon, if your puppy has had two or three good actions, give him his freedom and a meal. By night the dog's routine and the household routine should be back in their ruts—if life in any household with any puppy can ever be called a rut.

OTHER TYPES OF WORMS

There are several types of worms besides the roundworm, but the most common are the tapeworm, the hookworm, the whipworm and the filaria, or heartworm. The presence of

If life in any household with any puppy can ever be called a rut.

these worms is indicated by recognizable symptoms which I will describe for you under their various headings. These symptoms are important and should be watched out for, but in the final analysis there is only one definite way of knowing for sure whether a dog has any of these worms—and what kind—and that is by microscopic examination of his stool— or in the case of filariae, by microscopic examination of his blood and by X-ray; and all such examinations have to be done by a veterinarian. And treatment should be given or supervised by him; by supervised I mean that in some cases

—say, if a puppy is too young to take out to a veterinarian, or if a dog is too sick, or if you live outside a veterinarian's visiting range—a specimen of the dog's stool could be taken to him for examination, diagnosing and prescribing, and the worming done at home.

TAPEWORMS

In the adult dog, the ordinary tapeworm (there are a number of varieties) is the commonest of all worms, and the hardest to diagnose. I have seen innumerable cases of tapeworm infestation in which there was no outward evidence whatever and even microscopic examination failed to reveal the worms. So for the lay tapeworm sleuth I can only point out that tapeworms divide into segments; that it is these segments and not whole worms which pass out of the dog's rectum and that a segment which has been exposed to the outside world for a while looks like a dried-up grain of brown rice and a fresh arrival has a pinkish tinge. Tapeworm segments can often be seen around the base of the dog's tail, in his rectum and in his bedding. They sometimes wriggle out of the rectum of their own volition, and when this is happening the dog may drag his rectum along the floor in distress or make frenzied attempts to bite at it. When you see a dog doing this, examine his rectum for segments. The evidence is seeing them.

Dogs usually get tapeworms by swallowing such intermediary hosts as fleas and lice. It is also possible to get them from eating certain wildlife, such as rabbits and birds. The condition is treatable, but treatment should be administered professionally.

WHIPWORMS

The roundworm and the tapeworm are injurious to a dog's health because they take nourishment away from him

or clog up his intestines, but the whipworm (so called because it looks like a whip) burrows into the lining of the
caecum, absorbs blood and causes toxemia and inflammation.
A dog with whipworms has all the symptoms of roundworm
or tapeworm infestation, plus a couple more: blood is seen
intermittently in the stool, and the stool generally has an almost unbearably foul odor.

The caecum, a small section of the large intestine, is often
referred to as a dog's appendix. It is sometimes so badly
affected by whipworms that it has to be removed. This is the
operation you sometimes hear called "an operation for ap-
pendicitis." Dogs, I might add, do not have appendices.
Whipworms need professional attention.

HOOKWORMS

Like the whipworm, the hookworm burrows into the intestine and absorbs blood. The symptoms are general emaci-
ation; dull coat and eyes; vomiting and diarrhea, which is apt
to be bloody, and occasional convulsions.

FILARIAE

The filaria larvae and young worms are found in the blood
stream; the mature worm lodges mainly in the heart. The
chief symptoms are loss of weight, listlessness, occasional
convulsions, labored breathing, coughing and sometimes a
swelling of the legs. Microscopic examination of the blood
and X-ray are the only means of accurate diagnosis. Infestation with heartworms, the most vicious of the common
worms, can often be treated successfully by medical means
and by heart surgery.

For a long time filariae were found chiefly in the South,
where they were believed to be spread by mosquitoes and
ticks, but they are widely prevalent now and, regrettably,
seem to be increasing.

COCCIDIOSIS

Puppies are more susceptible than grown dogs to coccidiosis, which is indicated by a bloody stool and symptoms generally similar to those of distemper. It can be treated with sulfa drugs, but this is a matter for a veterinarian to handle. It is believed that coccidiosis develops under unsanitary conditions or that, at least, it thrives there.

GARLIC

There is a very, very old belief—more widely prevalent in European countries than here—that garlic is a cure for worms, and I have seen some mighty clean dogs whose owners claimed they were worm-free because they were given chopped garlic in their food—from a clove to three or four—every two months. Over the long years I have learned not to sneer at all of the old remedies and beliefs, as I was inclined to do when I first went into practice, because I have learned that some of them work, and I have seen some old-hat remedies discarded and retired only to be brought back years later with good results and high acclaim. Garlic is not one of the popular vermifuges today, but I can well believe that sizable and repeated servings of it would tend to discourage any worm from remaining in residence in a dog's intestine.

CHAPTER TEN

Fits

THERE ARE few experiences in amateur dog raising more alarming than the first fit. If your dog has a fit and you have never seen an animal in convulsions before, you will probably think the end has come—and not mercifully. The muscular spasms, the foaming at the mouth and the wild eyes are heartbreaking sights that none of us like to witness. But for the beginner it may be comforting to know that except in very unusual cases, relatively few dogs die during their first fit.

Fits are a warning, always, that something is wrong somewhere, and if you value your dog have him examined at once to find out what that something is. A fit may be the result of a minor disturbance like teething or fright. A fit may be the signal of oncoming distemper. A fit can be caused by a foreign object in the stomach or intestines—a nail maybe, or a fish bone. A fit may be caused by a heart lesion, a brain disturbance, worms, indigestion or, in the hot summertime, heat; and in bitches, a fit is sometimes the forerunner of menstruation. Fits are not for amateur diagnosticians.

TYPES OF FITS

Dogs in convulsions react in different ways. Some of them stiffen all over and champ at the jaws. Some fall over and kick the air with their feet. Some have running fits and rush blindly into doors, walls or chairs. Others stand still and bark hysterically. Some combine all the reactions. In all types of convulsions there is the unmistakable wild expression in the eyes, part or total unconsciousness and in nearly all cases frothing at the mouth and an involuntary elimination from the bowels and bladder. Fits last from a few seconds to ten or fifteen minutes and sometimes longer.

CARE OF THE DOG DURING A FIT

The first thing to do for the average fit is nothing. Just keep the dog as quiet as possible and leave him alone. Whatever you do, don't try to make him swallow anything—water or whisky, for example. In a convulsive state an animal is unable to swallow, and the liquid might choke him or go into his lungs.

If the fit is a running fit, in which the dog is in danger of injuring himself, throw a towel or a coat around him, or if he is a big dog, a blanket. The purpose of the covering is twofold: it is easier to hold a dog when he is covered, and the covering acts as a protection for your hands in case he tries to bite you, which he may very well do. If the dog is too big and strong for you to hold, don't try. Get out of the room and leave him alone until the fit is over.

CARE OF THE DOG AFTER A FIT

After the convulsions have subsided, the dog will probably be weak and wobbly on his legs. Stroke him gently and let him rest a few minutes. When he is somewhat calmed down, give him a barbiturate—a quarter of a grain to a grain and a half, depending on his size—or a tranquilizer. Don't feed him for several hours. Sometimes a dog will recover from one fit only to go into another a few minutes later. If this happens, call the veterinarian at once. In any case, always have a dog examined after a fit. Very little can be done for a dog during a fit, but there is no excuse for negligence afterward.

IF YOUR DOG HAS A FIT ON THE STREET

If your dog has a fit on the street, throw a coat over him and get him into a doorway, a small shop, a building lobby, or a taxi, if that is possible, and just sit there with him until the fit subsides. But get him off the street. The confusion and noise are bad for him, but worse than that is the possibility that his convulsions will be mistaken for rabies. The sight of a dog foaming at the mouth and the cry of "mad dog" from some hysterical bystander can cause havoc very quickly. If your dog should be imprudent enough to bite somebody at

Always have a dog examined after a fit.

such a time, he is liable to get shot by a policeman. All of this sounds very dire. Dogs have fits on the streets every day and very few of them come to any such calamitous end, particularly when they're on leashes. Nevertheless, such misfortunes can happen and have happened.

HEAT HYSTERIA AND HEAT PROSTRATION

Heat hysteria and heat prostration are both extremely serious. In hysteria the dog may become delirious, he may have convulsions and, as commonly happens, he may claw frantically at anything within his reach. I have seen dogs claw at things until their nails bled.

Heat prostration is seldom preceded by hysteria. The dog just becomes suddenly weak and falls over unconscious.

Lay treatment for either of these troubles is risky. Call a veterinarian immediately, and until he arrives do nothing but keep the dog as quiet as possible. Attempts to cool him off with ice packs or cool enemas—treatments frequently used—may help him, but on the other hand, there is the great risk of shock, which may cause death. Sponge his face and feet with cold water, use smelling salts and when he regains consciousness give him black coffee or whisky and water immediately. For the next few days keep him very quiet and feed him lightly on broths and milk.

Since heat prostration and heat hysteria are so dangerous, do everything you can to avoid them. During a heat wave, never take a dog out onto the street except in the early morning or late at night. Don't take puppies out at all. Fat dogs and old dogs should be kept indoors and as quiet and cool as possible. Sponge them off several times a day when the weather is unusually hot, and feed them lightly. Many dogs will refuse to eat anything at all during hot weather. Don't try to force them to eat. They know what they're doing.

CHAPTER ELEVEN

Distemper

WE HAVE come a long way since the days when gunpowder mixed with molasses was considered a specific for distemper; when a part of the treatment was a scalding-hot bath given every hour to "sweat the poisons out of the animal"; when tar was rubbed on the sufferer's nose so that he could inhale the fumes, which were believed to be curative. Even worse were the days of "bleeding" an animal, cutting the roof of the mouth and the lobes of the ears to "let out the bad blood"—which was once the veterinarian's cure-all (as well as the barber's for human ills). We have come a long way, but we have a way to go yet. There is still no specific for distemper.

Happily, however, it is not the dreaded disease today that it was ten years ago. This is mainly due to the fact that we know more generally about dogs. We know how to keep them in better health, and we know definitely that distemper in healthy dogs takes only a fraction of the toll that it does in anemic, wormy and rickety dogs. And today we have the antibiotics, which are by no means "sure cures" but certainly are miraculous combatants. And we have preventive inoculations and serums, which again, while not perfect, are so near

to it that it can be hoped with high confidence that the very
near future will see the goal reached. Maybe even tomorrow.

PREVENTION

More is known and more can be done about prevention
than about cure. We know that distemper attacks puppies,
but that it seldom attacks grown dogs and when it does, little
harm is done. We know that distemper is a virus disease and
that it is contagious. We know that a puppy can pick up the
germs not only from an infected dog but also from sidewalks,
lampposts, trees or anywhere an infected dog has been. We
know that a person nursing a case of distemper can carry the
germs on his clothes to another dog. We know that the germ
is airborne and, further, that a house or apartment where a
sick dog has been kept can harbor the germ for at least three
long months afterward. So if heretofore in this book I have
sounded over-fussy about keeping young puppies at home,
these are a few of the reasons.

On the brighter side, there are the preventive inoculations.
The permanent type of inoculation should not be given until
the puppy is around four months old and should be given
then only if he is in the best of health. This is most important. A wormy, anemic or rickety puppy, and particularly a
puppy with a fever, should not be given the permanent inoculation. Up to the age of two months, the temporary inoculations can be given. These are effective for short periods only
—about two weeks—and should be repeated that often. The
time durations, however, are gradually being increased as
these inoculations are being improved.

FIRST SYMPTOMS

The first symptoms of distemper are so varied, so numerous and so sly that every slightest indisposition in a puppy
might be looked upon as a potential forerunner of the disease. Because its approach is so insidious, it is often impossi-

ble even for a veterinarian to be sure in early diagnosis. Nevertheless, the chief symptoms are vomiting, diarrhea, convulsions, listlessness, refusal to eat, running eyes and nose, dry cough, continued shivering, a rise in temperature. A puppy may have one or two of these symptoms only. He may have them all. He may have none—except an elevated temperature.

Before going another step I want to stop right now to stress the necessity, the urgency, of understanding and using the thermometer. The theory that a dog's nose is his thermometer is complete foolishness. His nose can be hot when he is normal and cold when he is running a high temperature. A human rectal thermometer should be bought the day the dog is bought. As I have already said, but will say again, a dog's normal temperature is 101 degrees. As with humans, the normal point varies in different dogs, but not too much. In using the thermometer, grease it well, hold the dog still and insert it very gently into his rectum, leaving it there for whatever period of time instructions on the thermometer indicate. The length of time needed is the same for dogs as for humans.

All of the symptoms I have listed can be symptoms of common and inconsequential puppy upsets, and if you are the worrying type of dog owner, some of your worrying can be eased with a thermometer. Or it can be vindicated. If any of the listed symptoms is accompanied by a rise in temperature, or by a temperature that rises and falls, or if it persists, you might have cause for concern. If your puppy has an upset stomach, the sniffles or diarrhea or is uninterested in a meal, and if he has no fever, the chances are he is in no danger.

TREATMENT

There is no specific for distemper, but there are combatants. Distemper serums, effective only in the very early stages, and antibiotics given throughout are certainly helpful. A puppy with distemper symptoms should be put into the hands of a veterinarian at once. It and infectious hepatitis are diseases that no amateur should fool around with. And only if there is no veterinarian within a hundred miles of you do I suggest that you pay any attention whatever to the home treatments that I will suggest in the following paragraphs. They are only and strictly for owners who cannot for some reason find professional help.

Get the 100,000-unit penicillin tablets and give one twice a day for two or three days. If there seems to be no relief from the penicillin, switch to one of the other antibiotics of the mycin group: terramycin, Chloromycetin or aureomycin. For medium-sized dogs get the 250-milligram capsules and give one four times a day. For toys get the 50-milligram size and give four a day. For large breeds, give two of the 250-milligram capsules four times a day. Treatment should be continued for two or three days, or until the dog seems well out of danger—which may take a week or even two. Further treatment consists of treating the symptoms:

The eyes will probably be watery and sore. They should be bathed every two or three hours with cotton and warm 2-per cent boric acid solution, and if the eyelids become inflamed, gently massage 1-per cent yellow mercuric oxide ointment into them twice a day.

The nose should be kept open and free. Clean it inside and out with cotton and boric acid solution as frequently as is necessary, and twice a day tilt the dog's head back and drop a few drops of Argyrol or plain mineral oil into each nostril. Dogs' noses are highly sensitive and many of them hate nose drops. Some will practically go into hysterics at the sight of a nose dropper. If your dog feels this way about the matter, let him have his way. Hysterics are as hard on the constitution as a running or stopped-up nose.

Ulcers sometimes appear in the mouth, and the teeth may become coated with a brownish fuzz. Wash the mouth out daily with warm bicarbonate of soda solution and cotton.

When the respiratory tract is affected, the dog will have trouble breathing and will have spasms of coughing. Rub his chest briskly and for several minutes at a time with camphorated oil. This will relieve the congestion to some extent, and the fumes from the oil will make breathing easier. Eucalyptus oil in steaming water held under the dog's nose is another aid to breathing.

When there has been persistent diarrhea, the rectum will probably be sore and tender. Bathe it with boric acid solution and put Vaseline on it two or three times a day. Because of the frequency and urgency of evacuation, the puppy may not always be able to get to his paper or box in time, but don't scold him. He can't help it, and scolding will only make him feel worse. Further treatment for diarrhea is described in the following chapter, as is vomiting, another distemper disturbance.

Running fits are seldom seen in distemper, and it is only in running fits that the dog is likely to injure himself. In distemper the dog generally falls over on one side and twitches and champs at the mouth, or he may stand and champ at the mouth. Leave him absolutely alone. Any fussing around will only aggravate the condition. After he has recovered, give him a quarter to half a grain of phenobarbital or whatever sedative you have around the house, or whisky in water. Fits are alarming and unquestionably serious manifestations of the disease, but I have seen dogs in distemper have as many as twelve and fifteen fits a day and recover without a single aftereffect.

GENERAL NURSING

Warmth is one of the first considerations. If the weather is cold or even chilly, put a sweater on the dog—the kind that covers his chest and throat—and leave it on him for the duration of the disease. Keep him out of drafts, and at night, if the heat is turned off, put an extra sweater on him, or put an electric pad under his bedding. (Don't try to put an electric pad next to him; the heat will make him uncomfortable and he will leave the bed.) If he absolutely refuses to relieve himself in the house on papers, put an additional coat on him and take him out, but only long enough for his functions.

Raw beef is the best nourishment for a dog in sickness or in health. Very often in sickness, however, a dog will refuse it altogether. If he does, cook the meat slightly. If this fails to tempt him, try chicken, fish, eggs, milk or cereal. In fact, give him anything that seems to appeal to him: tomato juice, broths, fruits, vegetables, canned food—anything that might tempt his finicky appetite; and dogs often develop peculiar appetites during illness. I had a patient recently who ate nothing for ten days but condensed milk. He had never before liked condensed milk, but during his illness he would touch nothing else. I had another who ate nothing but canned tomatoes for two weeks, though his owner did manage to smuggle beef juice into them. That is one of the advantages of finding something a dog will eat: you can always sneak something else into it to make it more nutritive. Cod-liver oil is always an excellent vitality builder. Give him a quarter tablespoonful a day, or give him the capsules. If it doesn't agree with him, if he vomits it up, don't give him any more. Vitamin tablets should be increased during illness. If you have been giving one a day, give two or three. Whisky or brandy diluted with water is a good appetite stimulant. I have seen many dogs kept alive on whisky, the white of an egg and milk.

Since nourishment is such an important part of the distemper treatment, try all sorts of tricks to get the dog to eat. Move his dish to another part of the house if he is accustomed, say, to eating in the kitchen. The kitchen odors may upset him. Feed him by hand or with a spoon. Hand feeding

Move his dish to another part of the house.

is one of the commonest solutions. Many dogs will eat out of their owner's hand when they won't touch food out of a dish. Feeding from the table at your own mealtime is another trick that sometimes works. A dog will often take an interest in food that you eat and will eat bits that are given him from your own plate. During distemper is no time to worry about spoiling a dog and getting him into bad habits.

Hand feeding is one of the commonest solutions.

If the dog refuses every kind of food and every manner of coaxing, he must be force-fed. This is done with liquids—broths, beef extract, milk, whisky and water, fruit juices and so on. Tilt the dog's head back a little and pull his lips out to the side. This will form a pocket. Slowly pour the liquid into this pocket, giving the dog a chance to swallow after each tablespoonful or two. A small bottle is more practical than a spoon.

KEEPING THE DOG'S SPIRITS UP

The general idea in treating distemper is to try to keep up the dog's vitality so that he can hold his own against the disease until it has run its course. His symptoms are eased with medicines, he is fed nourishing foods and he is kept warm and comfortable all toward this end. But that is not enough. Dogs get depressed in illness. They suffer real depressions. The heart is depressed, the pulse retarded, the whole system becomes sluggish and noncombative and the patient is likely to give up. I have seen many dogs die from what could be diagnosed only as "giving up." In illness they need a lot of cheering up from the people they know and trust—back

Dogs suffer from depression.

rubs, kind words and their presence in the room for as much time as they can spare. When a sick dog is left alone for too long, his spirits sag.

Hospitals are certainly much better equipped to handle sickness than homes. They offer every comfort, they provide up-to-date medical and surgical treatment and they are prepared for any last-minute emergency measures such as oxygen tents, blood transfusions and intravenous injections. But there is no treatment—sometimes no hope even—for a dog who is miserable away from his folks. All hospital people are well aware that there are dogs who will pine away or give up more easily in the hospital than at home, and when they see a case going this way, they will urge the owners to take the dog home.

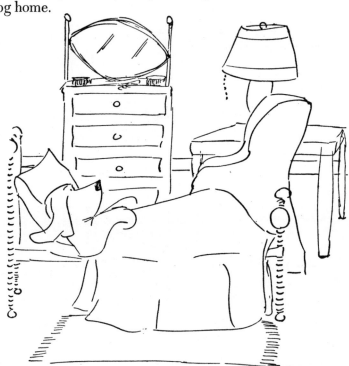

The dog will be calmer at home.

There are dogs, on the other hand, who continue merry no matter where they are or what they have. Many a dog too, I am sure, thinks he is sicker than he really is.

AFTEREFFECTS OF DISTEMPER

The aftereffects of distemper are often disheartening, and there is almost nothing the layman can do. Chorea, or St. Vitus' dance as it's popularly called, is the commonest of them. With it the patient may twitch all over, or it may affect only one part—one eyelid perhaps, one leg, possibly the abdominal muscles. Depending on the severity of the case, the dog may or may not get over it.

Blindness and paralysis are likewise common aftermaths, and depending on the severity of the affliction and the dog's recuperative ability, they can or cannot be treated successfully. I have seen many cases of distemper blindness pass off after a month or two, and many severe case of paralysis cured.

Inability to control the bladder and the bowels is still another common aftereffect, as is a dry cough which may persist for weeks or months. These troubles can usually be treated successfully.

Disheartening and discouraging as some of the aftereffects of distemper are, I would hesitate a long time before having a dog destroyed, as is too often recommended. Too often dog owners give up when they know their dogs are suffering from chorea, meningitis, paralysis or blindness, because it is a common belief that there is no hope for them. As long as there's life there's hope is my stand in these days of wonderful research and new and miraculous discoveries just around the corner.

CHAPTER TWELVE

Other Common Ailments

INFECTIOUS HEPATITIS

INFECTIOUS HEPATITIS, a virus that affects the liver, is almost as widely prevalent as distemper. Like distemper it affects puppies chiefly and is found in older dogs only occasionally. An early and distinctive symptom of this disease is a profound lethargy, bordering on collapse, and the puppy will probably withdraw from all human contact and lie hidden in some dark place. Other early symptoms may be a painful abdomen and a tendency to walk in a tucked-in manner and with a peculiar curving of the back. Other symptoms that may be manifest are the same as the ones described under DISTEMPER, the two diseases being frequently mistaken for each other. The dog can also have the two diseases concurrently. Fever is almost invariably present, running as a rule from 103 to 106 degrees.

There is no home treatment for infectious hepatitis. There are ways to treat it—some highly effective ways—but they must be done by a veterinarian. And a veterinarian should be called early, as the disease is a fast-moving one. As its name makes clear, it is infectious among dogs, so don't let your dog go near a known case of it. Preventive inoculations given in puppyhood, along with distemper and leptospirosis inoculations, are of enormous help.

LEPTOSPIROSIS

This disease can be treated with antibiotics, but the best method of dealing with it is the preventive one of immunizing shots given in puppyhood. They are given along with the distemper and hepatitis shots and can be repeated every six months.

Leptospirosis is spread by a spirochete in the urine of an infected dog or rat, usually through direct contact, but sometimes through drinking of contaminated water. The symptoms are similar to those of distemper, with the sometimes distinguishing symptom of tiny red spots in the mouth. But diagnosis and treatment for leptospirosis is for a veterinarian. The owner's responsibility is to see that his dog gets the immunizing shots and to get professional help for him if he seems sick for no traceable reason.

MENINGITIS

Meningitis is a serious inflammation of the coverings of the brain and spinal cord. The dog suffering from it may have difficulty in walking, and one of the characteristics of the disease is that he will usually walk around in circles in a stupor or semistupor. He may whine a great deal or become extremely timid, and his eyesight may become impaired. There is nothing the amateur can do. As serious as meningitis is, I have seen some dogs cured of it. Like chorea, though, it is a long, lingering ailment.

BLUE EYE

This is one of the commonest of all eye troubles. The white of the eye usually turns red, and the cornea (or the coat that covers the iris and the pupil of the eye) turns a bluish white.

Blue eye often accompanies distemper, hepatitis or other internal disorders, but it can be the result of some external irritation. Bathe the eye with warm 2-per cent boric acid solution and cotton several times a day; twice a day put a drop or two of 5-per cent Argyrol into the eye, or apply 1-per cent yellow mercuric oxide ointment. Argyrol should not be used for more than two or three days in a row, because it becomes irritating if the treatment is prolonged, and it causes discoloration. Try the steroid preparations.

INFLAMED HARDER'S GLAND

Harder's gland is found on the inside corner of the eye. When the haw, or third eyelid, becomes inflamed, the gland reddens and swells, sometimes covering nearly half the eye. Sometimes a drop or two of Argyrol will relieve the trouble, or one of the steroid preparations. More often the swelling recurs and recurs and becomes chronic, and there is nothing to do about it but have the gland removed surgically.

INVERTED EYELIDS

This condition is found commonly among English bulls, chows, great Danes and St. Bernards, but many other breeds also suffer from it. Many dogs are born with it. Surgery is usually the only solution, and the quicker done the better, as the eye can ultimately be destroyed by the irritation it produces. Thanks to intelligent breeding, this trouble, happily, is disappearing.

STIES

Treat sties with warm boric acid compresses until they come to a head and break. If they don't break of their own accord, squeeze them gently. Afterward apply 1-per cent yellow oxide ointment twice a day for a week or ten days.

CATARACTS

Cataracts are opacities that appear on the lens, which is just back of the pupil of the eye, and spread until the whole lens is affected and blindness results. The prognosis for cataract is not favorable. Occasionally, dependent upon the kind and cause, cataracts can be cured, but only occasionally. They can be removed surgically for the sake of appearance, but except in certain forms the operation seldom improves the sight of the eye. If a dog could be fitted with glasses afterward, the operation could be made practicable, as it is with humans, but I have never heard of a dog who would put up with glasses. Except one whom I will tell you about in a minute. Older dogs are more susceptible to cataract, and as the growth is slow, they seldom reach the total-blindness stage. I have seen several cases, however, in dogs under a year old.

CONJUNCTIVITIS

This is an inflammation of the inner lining of the eyelid and part of the eyeball. It can be caused by dust, smoke, a scratch, a foreign substance or some internal disturbance. And it frequently occurs among dogs who ride for long distances in cars with their heads sticking out the window like locomotive engineers.

I had one of these engineers once as a patient. He belonged to a bachelor who worked in New York and lived on Long Island and commuted by car every day. The dog commuted with him every day, always with his head sticking out the window. He developed a bad case of conjunctivitis, and I advised the owner either to leave the dog at home or to keep the car windows closed.

He followed my advice for two days. He left the dog at home the first day. That night his landlord reported that the dog had howled all day long, and had refused to eat, had refused to go out and instead used the floor as a toilet and had tried to bite the landlord every time he went near him. The next day the owner took the dog with him and kept the car windows closed. The dog moped all day.

The third day the owner had him fitted up with goggles, and that evening Casey was back at the throttle, whizzing happily across the Queensborough Bridge. He wore the goggles for six months to my knowledge and probably longer—I lost track of him (he probably got a real job with the B & O or the Pennsylvania or somewhere)—but he is the only dog I know of who ever stuck with glasses, or treated them in any way except to paw them off.

I have seen vaudeville dogs trained to wear lensless glasses, but corrective glasses (and it has been tried), no; not so far, that is, but maybe in time. I also remember seeing a picture once of one of the early balloon ascensions, and in the middle of the group of ascenders, all wearing dusters and goggles, there he was—a small terrier posing it up big, wearing goggles and looking very intrepid.

The treatment for conjunctivitis is as follows: Bathe the eye with cotton and 2-per cent boric acid solution two or three times a day, and twice a day squeeze a little 1-per cent yellow mercuric oxide ointment into the eyes, or one of the sulfa ointments, or an antibiotic ophthalmic.

EAR TROUBLES

The ear is an intricate organ, affected by various internal and external conditions. A treatment that will ease many of the minor troubles is as follows: Wipe the ear out with cotton and peroxide but only as far as your finger will reach; don't probe too far. Then wipe out thoroughly with dry cotton. If the ear is discharging, dust boric acid into it. If it is dry and scaly, apply olive oil or camphorated oil. If inflamed, use Nupercainal ointment, or one of the antibiotic ointments. If inflammation does not subside, get professional help.

Dogs can, without doubt, be in great pain from ear troubles. They will shake their heads, paw at the ear, rub it up against something and run around in circles in distress. One small flea, however, or a small cake of dirt or dust in the ear will bring on reactions just as frenzied. They think they are dying. If you see your dog carrying on in this fashion, always examine his ears. If you find the irritant, remove it, of course; if you don't, drop a few drops of warm olive oil or glycerine deep into the ear and massage all around the base of the ear.

EAR MITES

A black, caked material in the ear canal, if accompanied by scratching and a great deal of head shaking, may well indicate ear mites. Clean the ear out twice a day with ether and cotton and apply two per cent yellow mercuric oxide ointment. Don't use any of the insecticides in the ear—the ones commonly used for fleas, lice and ticks—because they are too strong and will cause inflammation.

VOMITING

Because of their feeble-mindedness about eating anything and everything that comes their way, dogs let themselves in for all kinds of stomach upsets. Many of these upsets are minor. The dog eats something undesirable, the stomach rebels, vomiting follows and that's all there is to it. Any dog should be allowed to vomit once or twice with no questions asked. If he continues, though, try to diagnose the trouble. Continued vomiting can mean worms or a foreign object in the stomach or throat; it can be a symptom of oncoming distemper, hepatitis or other diseases or it can be due to poisoning, constipation or kidney disorder.

The treatment, of course, depends upon the cause, but the first step in any case is to take the dog off food for twenty-four hours. Don't give him water, either: just cracked ice occasionally.

The next step is to clean out his system and quiet his stomach down. Give him an enema and a dose of milk of magnesia. If he vomits up the milk of magnesia, don't repeat it—just give the enema. Use warm water for this with bicarbonate of soda, a teaspoonful to a pint. Use any ordinary human rectal syringe or an infant-sized one, depending on the size of the dog.

To settle his stomach, give rhubarb and soda or milk of bismuth; follow with a little whisky or a tranquilizer. This treatment should be given every two hours (omitting the tranquilizer) until the vomiting stops. If it doesn't stop and the dog seems to be weakening fast, or if there is blood in the vomitus, or if the vomitus is black or a dark brownish green, or if there is fever, get professional help at once.

Vomiting as a result of poisoning or swallowing of foreign objects is described in the chapter on HOUSEHOLD ACCIDENTS. Vomiting as a symptom of other troubles is described under the respective troubles: DISTEMPER, WORMS and so on.

DIARRHEA

Like vomiting, diarrhea can be symptomatic of many things: worms, distemper, foreign objects, incorrect feeding, poisons, nervous disorders, ordinary everyday upsets and constipation or hardening of the intestinal contents.

Also like vomiting, diarrhea is a negligible complaint unless it continues for, say, twenty-four or twenty-eight hours, or it recurs frequently, or there is blood in the stool, or fever.

Ordinary diarrhea can usually be cleared up in a couple of days with Kaopectate—a teaspoonful to a tablespoonful every two hours. You can also give ten drops of paregoric in water every three or four hours. All food and water should be withheld for twenty-four hours, with barley water or cracked ice given occasionally. Afterward give only solid foods with boiled rice or boiled or baked potato added.

CONSTIPATION

Milk of magnesia, in my opinion, is one of the best and safest all-around laxatives. Depending on the size of the dog, give a quarter teaspoonful to a tablespoonful in the morning. Cascara sagrada is another good laxative. Give a five-grain tablet in the morning on an empty stomach, or half a tablet to small dogs. (By no means give a dog the cascara compound that humans use. It contains strychnine.)

If immediate relief is needed, use glycerin suppositories (infant or adult size) or enemas. Enemas are described in this chapter under the paragraph on VOMITING.

For chronic constipation, add more roughage to the dog's diet and mix from a teaspoonful to a tablespoonful of mineral oil in his food daily. And see that he gets plenty of exercise; lack of exercise is a common cause of constipation. Also change the dog's diet; if he has been eating beef, try lamb or mutton or mix a little liver or kidneys in with his beef. Do not allow a chronic case of constipation to run too long without consulting a veterinarian. The dog may be suffering from a tumor, from a foreign object or from something else that may be acting as an obstruction.

Hardening of the intestinal contents is a fairly common trouble. The dog will strain and strain and be able to pass nothing or else only a watery material. Give large doses of mineral oil and then give a warm mineral-oil or saline enema and massage the abdomen. You may have to repeat the enema several times before the contents are softened up enough to pass, and it may be necessary for a veterinarian to remove the cementlike material by instrument.

Very often a dog may be suffering from constipation for no reason other than the caking of fecal material around the rectum. Examine him for this, and if such is the case, remove it with warm water and soap.

Never give a dog laxative pills (or any kind of medicine

prescribed for humans) unless you are quite sure of all the ingredients in them. Several of the laxatives contain strychnine, which even in very small doses is often fatal to dogs.

Rainy and snowy days have a constipating effect on some dogs. You can walk your feet off with them and nothing will happen. For such cases, use a glycerin suppository a few minutes before the walk.

ASTHMA

Most cases of cardiac and bronchial asthma are incurable, but a few things can be done to make the patient more comfortable. Obesity is an aggravation, and the sufferer should be dieted if he is overweight. Calcium lactate, a quarter to half a teaspoonful given twice a day, is a good tonic. Don't allow the patient to become constipated, and don't exercise him too much or allow him to get too excited, as these conditions bring on attacks. The asthma attack is characterized by coughing, wheezing and labored breathing. Some of the mentholated vapor inhalants on the market are useful during attacks; whisky or brandy diluted in water is often helpful, and a sedative will help quiet the patient down. Human attention, such as gentle patting and rubbing and a soothing talking to, are of great comfort and reassurance to the sufferer, since fear always accompanies an attack. Bronchial and cardiac asthma are common ailments in old dogs, particularly Pomeranians, French and English bulls and the toy breeds. Digitalis, antihistamines and cortisone are helpful to the patient, but these should be given only on the advice of and under the direction of your veterinarian.

TEETHING

Teething presents few problems. The baby teeth begin to fall out around the fourth or fifth month, and the new set is generally complete at the sixth month. Teething seems to be slower in the small and toy dogs. Puppies frequently swallow their first teeth. This is nothing to worry about; the teeth are soft, and the stomach is perfectly capable of handling the matter. All teething puppies should be given something to chew on, and there is nothing better than a shank bone or knucklebone. Occasionally, but not often, puppies have fits from teething; see the chapter on FITS. But be sure the fit is due to teething and not to something more serious.

Care of the teeth generally is being given more and more attention, as it is well known that "clean as a hound's tooth" was thought up by somebody who didn't know hounds' teeth. Dental flossing and brushing are daily routines with quite a few dogs nowadays, and there are even mouth washes for the really fastidious. In time there will undoubtedly be dog dentists. Cleaning the tartar off the teeth is now a fairly common practice with veterinarians. A few dogs have to be completely anesthetized for this as for other dental work, such as tooth pulling and filling. Even the toughest of dogs is no stoic who will sit in a dentist's chair and put up with any local anesthetic. Filling is not widely practiced as yet, nor is capping. I know a Pekingese, though, who has a gold tooth. He is, incidentally, one of the meanest animals I have ever known, and when he bares that gold tooth it is not to show it off, nor is he smiling. When you see those lips start to curl back, you duck.

RETENTION OF URINE

This may be caused by irregular habits (if a dog has to wait for a long time he may be unable to void); obesity; cystitis; chill; bladder, kidney or urethral stones; genital disorders or a toxic condition. Give ten drops of sweet spirits of niter in two teaspoonfuls of water every half hour until three doses have been given. Or if you have urotropin around, give him a five-grain tablet dissolved in water (half a tablet for small dogs). If the cause is a minor one, the patient should be normal within a few hours. This treatment can be used for dogs who have rainy-day trouble as described under CONSTIPATION. Prolonged retention of urine should be called to your veterinarian's attention.

BLADDER STONES

Retention of the urine is a common symptom of bladder stones. Strain and pain accompany frequent efforts at voiding, and blood is sometimes seen in the urine. Blood in the urine can be due to strain, a toxic condition or an internal injury or complication of some part of the genito-urinary tract. The patient suffering from bladder stones will generally walk stiff-legged, with his back arched in obvious pain. An operation is usually necessary for this, but temporary relief can be achieved with the following: Give two and a half grains of urotropin dissolved in one tablespoon of water every two hours. Apply warm damp cloths to the lower back and the abdomen. Press the walls of the abdomen, but by all means press them very gently, as it is possible to rupture a full bladder if too much or too sudden pressure is used. If the stones are small they can sometimes be flushed or pressed out in this way.

ANAL ABSCESSES

Anal abscesses, or hemorrhoids, as they're popularly called, are painful swellings that appear on the sides of the rectum, and during the course of their run the dog is in no way apt to be happy. He will drag his rectum along the floor or make frantic efforts to bite at it, or cry out at times, and defecation is often so painful to him that he is liable to give up any attempt at it. If this happens he must be given a laxative; constipation will aggravate the trouble.

Once the abscesses have formed, there is nothing much to do for them but wait until they come to a head and break of their own accord, or have them lanced. They can be brought to a head perhaps a little sooner and the pain can be alleviated slightly by the application of warm boric acid packs several times a day and 10-per cent Ichthyol ointment twice a day.

In stubborn and recurrent cases, the anal glands can be treated by a periodic expressing and massage method. If this fails, they should be removed surgically. Certain forms of skin trouble, interestingly enough, have also been known to be helped by this operation.

PROLAPSED RECTUM

This occurs in puppies more often than in older dogs. An inch or more of the intestine will protrude from the anus. Bathe it with a mild antiseptic, grease it with Vaseline and gently push it back into place. Apply cotton saturated with boric acid solution to the rectum and hold it there for a few minutes. Keep the dog very quiet for several hours. Give him a sedative.

SCREW-TAIL IRRITATIONS

Boston terriers and other dogs that wear screw tails are liable to suffer from irritation under the tail. The affected parts should be treated twice a day with 5-per cent tannic acid and salicylic acid in alcohol, or any mild antiseptic, and have powder dusted over them. Bismuth formic iodide powder is also good. Five per cent boric acid ointment should be used if the parts seem hard and crusted.

HIP DYSPLASIA

This is a problem of concern in the dog world and one on which wide and intensive research is being done. It is an ailment in which the thigh bones pull away from the hip sockets and a degeneration of the femoral heads and the sockets ensues. It occurs almost exclusively in the larger breeds, with no indication of anything's being amiss with the dog until he is around six months old or, more often, a year old. X-ray up to these months will show nothing wrong. Occasionally, but only occasionally, the trouble will show up at three or four months. The symptoms are a stiffening of the gait and pain. There are mild cases and severe cases. Surgery has been used, but it is, so far, not the answer. Selective breeding is being practiced scrupulously in reputable kennels and by responsible breeders as one way to try to eliminate hip dysplasia, as it is possibly, or probably, hereditary.

RICKETS

Rickets is a disease of the bones of young dogs caused by calcium deficiency. Insufficient food can cause it, and the wrong kind of food, or the animal's inability to assimilate his food properly.

An irregular development of the bones is the commonest symptom. The bones of the head and jaw may bulge, giving the dog a deformed look, but the legs are the most generally affected. They bow, and the joints are enlarged and sore to the touch—so much so that in some cases the dog is unable to walk. Further symptoms that may be associated with rickets are poor coat, dull eyes, listlessness and a bloated stomach.

When treated early enough, rickets can be cured by a diet of meat, eggs, milk, cod-liver oil, calcium lactate and large doses of all-purpose vitamins with additional and large doses of Vitamins A and D. The dog should also have plenty of sunshine if possible, and be kept fairly quiet, because rickety bones will fracture easily.

PARALYSIS

Paralysis is usually a symptom and not a disease. It is brought on by injury to the nervous system, and unless the injury is unusually severe, the chances are the dog will get over it. I have had several cases of paralysis due to fractured backs—which certainly is about as serious an injury as there is—and the patients recovered. Paralysis due to distemper is serious but not necessarily incurable. Paralysis due to a cerebral hemorrhage can also, in some cases, be successfully treated. Though the affliction is pitiable to see, a great deal can be done for it nowadays with massage, electrical vibrations, violet-ray and short-wave treatments and corrective medicines.

HALITOSIS

Have the teeth examined and the tartar deposits and any decayed teeth removed. If this is not effective, the trouble may be in the stomach. Give the dog three or four charcoal tablets a day, or a quarter teaspoonful of bicarbonate of soda in his food twice a day and a little limewater in his drinking water. Constipation may be the cause, or there may be a foreign substance in his throat, wedged between his teeth or embedded in his mouth somewhere. If none of these seems to be the cause, have the tonsils examined. They may be diseased, necessitating either treatment or removal.

DENTAL FISTULA

Often a discharging wound will appear half an inch or an inch below the eye, sometimes under both eyes. This is caused by an infected molar tooth, and the only treatment is extraction of the tooth.

DISEASES OF THE REPRODUCTIVE ORGANS

Diseases of the reproductive organs are so complicated and so mixed up with the urinary tract that I feel it would be futile in a book of this type to go into any long and involved description of the dozens of various troubles and symptoms; many genital and urinary troubles, to confuse matters further, even have identical symptoms. Such an undertaking would do little toward enlightening the amateur dog owner, and getting it all down would kill me, so we will stick to the simpler troubles and the simpler treatments.

In the bitch many disorders are indicated by a swelling and irritation of the vulva and by a discharge and difficulty in urinating. A blanket treatment for most genital troubles is an antiseptic douche. This will tend to relieve irritation and correct inflammation if it hasn't gone too far, or unless there is a tumor or complication that only surgery will relieve. One of the best douches is made with warm water and potassium permanganate. This preparation comes in five-grain tablets. Use about six tablets to a pint of warm water, and give from two to four douches a day. Use a human rectal syringe or an infant-size one, depending on the size of the dog. Insert the nozzle an inch into the vagina—not too far, just barely into it. For discharging troubles of any kind, I suggest the use of a sanitary pad. This will keep the bitch from injuring herself in her attempts at relief by biting, scratching and rubbing, and also it will protect the household furnishings.

In the male dog many disorders are indicated by a swelling of the penis or testicles; a discharge, sometimes bloody; difficulty in urinating; blood in the urine and walking with a stiff-legged, straddling gait. These symptoms can mean a dozen different troubles, urinary or genital. But relief for the male also can often be achieved with an antiseptic douche. This is done with an ordinary human ear syringe. Insert the nozzle into the prepuce about half an inch and use warm water and potassium permanganate as prescribed for bitches.

The genital parts of dogs and bitches should always be kept clean. In this way many later and more serious developments can be avoided. Wash the parts regularly with a mild antiseptic solution of some kind—plain bicarbonate of soda solution is good enough—and at the first indication of swelling or discharge, use the douche.

Male and female hormones are now proved boons for many genitary and secondary ailments, as are many of the antibiotics, and recovery from many disorders long considered hopeless is now a daily occurrence. Administration of any of the hormone group is still a tricky treatment, and under no circumstances should they be given without professional advice.

CANCER

You may have heard, and there are many who believe, that there is no such thing as cancer in dogs. Dogs definitely get cancer. They get cancer of the breast, the bone, the skin, the jaw, the rectum—everywhere, in fact, that human beings get it. And symptoms are about the same; lumps should be examined, loss of weight checked, and after middle age regular checkups would be wise. Cancer is found in young dogs too, but not often. Caught early, it can often be successfully treated—chiefly by surgery.

TUBERCULOSIS

This is seldom found in dogs. A chronic cough, which many owners worry about and believe is tuberculosis, can be due to many things—maybe the dog smokes too much, for one—but the chances are it is not due to tuberculosis. The rare cases of it can be cured.

CHAPTER THIRTEEN

Accidents in the City Household

FOREIGN OBJECTS IN THE STOMACH

By "foreign objects" I mean such doubtfully nourishing items as nails, glass, bathtub stoppers, stones, beer caps, rubber, wire, combs and other similar fare that seems to appeal to most puppies. One meal of nails or beer caps will sometimes cure a puppy forever of experimenting around, but most of them will keep right at it until they outgrow the tendency or until God takes them home to heaven with a stomach full of hardware. There is a Scotty bitch in our hospital at this writing who has never learned that there are things in this world that cannot be digested, and she is over a year old. During the past year we have removed from her stomach, which at times has resembled a plumber's kit, the following assortment of tidbits: one lot of four nails, a foot of electric wiring, an electric plug, a brooch, a rubber Mickey Mouse, one lot of stones, a wine-glass stem and a key ring with three keys on it. One of our most frequent visitors, she is affectionately known around the hospital as Satchel.

A dog's stomach is an astoundingly tough organ, and it can digest, or at least pass on, some unbelievable things (Satchel's stomach is made of some substance so bizarre it would baffle the Du Pont laboratories), but it is better not to trust that toughness too far. Dog's stomachs are as capricious as their appetites; they may swallow and eliminate half a dozen nails without a scratch and have to be operated on for a piece of rubber. Rubber, in fact, is one of the most dangerous things a dog can swallow. It sticks to a dog's insides. A good third of our foreign-object operations are for rubber toys of the soft type—rubber cats, balls and mice.

I am afraid there is no cure except time for the fey appetites of puppies. They outgrow it eventually, but while you're waiting for time, you might keep everything smaller than a trunk out of the puppy's reach and try to divert him with harmless and valueless playthings of his own. Men's old shoes are good playthings, and there is nothing that will get a dog's mind off lampshades and floor plugs quicker than a shank bone or a knucklebone. Some of the heavier rubber toys are all right provided you take them away if they show signs of softening or weakening. Hard or simulated rubber gives a dog a lot of pleasure; it is tough enough to act as a challenge to him and compliant enough to make him think he is getting somewhere in life. For man or beast you can't beat that combination.

In spite of all the precautions in the world, an ingenious puppy can always ferret out something somewhere that is dangerous to swallow, so I give you herewith a first-aid treatment to be used in such crises. This treatment is to be used only immediately after or a short time after the foreign object or objects have been swallowed.

FIRST-AID TREATMENT FOR REMOVING FOREIGN OBJECTS FROM THE STOMACH

Give the dog a large meal of something soft—bread is a good thing. Then put a couple of teaspoonfuls of salt on the back of his tongue (but don't stop to measure it). This should make him vomit. Rarely will salt fail, but if it should, try warm mustard water. If the object comes up in vomiting, naturally you needn't repeat the dose, but if it doesn't, or if you are in any doubt as to whether you have got up the whole of it—in the case of glass, for example—wait a few minutes and give another dose of salt. If in a few hours the dog shows signs of distress—if he has a watery diarrhea or if his stomach or abdomen is swollen or sore to the touch—give him a dose of mineral oil: from a tablespoonful or two to half a cup, depending on the size of the dog. If he is still in pain after the lubrication, or if there should be blood in his stool or urine, have him fluoroscoped or X-rayed.

If, unknown to you, the dog swallows something dangerous, the symptoms will be prolonged or recurring attacks of vomiting or diarrhea, or both, or convulsive griping, and his stomach or abdomen will be sore. Or, as sometimes happens, a foreign object will get lodged in a dog's throat or stomach and stay lodged for as long as a month or two with no outward symptoms except possibly a loss of weight and intermittent vomiting. There is very little the amateur can safely do about foreign objects once the first-aid stage is passed.

FIRST-AID TREATMENT FOR REMOVING FOREIGN OBJECTS FROM THE MOUTH OR THROAT

A dog with a foreign object in his tongue, teeth, mouth, or throat (usually a bone splinter, or a needle or pin) will try to cough it up or rub his mouth and throat with his paw and shake his head a lot. If in great pain he may become hysterical.

Open the dog's mouth. A sure way to get a dog's mouth open is to put your palm over the dog's muzzle and press the sides of his lips against his teeth with your fingers on one side and your thumb on the other. This will force his mouth open. Examine his mouth carefully; look between his teeth, and at his tongue on top and underneath. Pull his tongue out as far as you can, using a handkerchief to hold it, and look down his throat. If you see the object and if it is not too deeply embedded, pull it out with your fingers or with tweezers. If it is too far embedded to pull out, or if there is danger of its breaking off in the pulling, see a veterinarian. If you don't find anything and the dog continues to choke, tries to vomit or paws his mouth, have him X-rayed.

ELECTRIC SHOCKS

Now and then a puppy will chew into an electric wire and be knocked out. If this happens, give him a whiff of ammonia and, when he comes to, a little whisky in water or black coffee. If his mouth is burned, put strong tea on the burn. If the shock should be great enough to stop the dog's breathing, press in and out on his ribs just back of his front legs and wave a piece of cotton saturated with ammonia under his nose. Severe cases of shock from ordinary wiring are fairly rare.

FALLS

If bones are broken you will know it. The dog will limp or refuse to walk, and you may be able to tell where the break is by feeling around the dog: you can feel the break or feel a grating of the bones. You can also get your hand bitten in the process. Dogs in pain will often bite. Internal injuries are more deceptive. A dog can be seriously hurt internally and not show a sign of it for twenty-four hours afterward, when he may suddenly have a hemorrhage from the mouth, nose, rectum or bladder. Whether a dog shows any immediate signs of distress or not, a really bad fall can be serious, and the dog should be kept bed-quiet with sedatives for at least two days. Don't feed him for the first twenty-four hours.

CUTS

If the cut is mild, put some peroxide or boric acid on it and forget about it. If the cut is deep, put a packing of cotton and gauze on it, saturate it with boric acid and bandage it up rather tightly but not so tightly that circulation will be stopped. If the cut is serious and hemorrhaging, hold a heavy boric acid packing against the wound as tightly as you can until you can get the wound sutured by a veterinarian. If the hemorrhage is on the foot or leg, put a tourniquet above it (taking care not to make the tourniquet too tight, and easing it gently every few minutes) until you can get help.

PAINT POISONING

White-lead poisoning can be serious, and if there is any great amount of painting going on around the house, the dog should be taken away somewhere until it is over. Even if he doesn't actually drink the paint out of the bucket, he can sometimes get a dose of poisoning by breathing the fumes of the paint. Or by drinking water that has been in a room with the fumes. The treatment for this is forced vomiting induced by a couple of teaspoonfuls of salt on the back of the tongue. After vomiting, give the white of an egg and milk.

ARSENIC POISONING

Arsenic is the basis of most rat poisonings, and the first-aid treatment is the same as for paint poisoning.

STRYCHNINE

Strychnine is one of the deadliest of poisons for dogs. A sixtieth of a grain can be fatal to a small dog, so if you have any medicines containing strychnine around the house, keep them locked up. If you catch a dog eating or drinking a medicine that has strychnine in it, empty his stomach immediately as described in the foregoing paragraphs and give him the white of an egg. Immediate treatment can sometimes save a dog.

INJURED TAIL

A bruised tail can be treated with boric acid packs or Epsom salts packs. If the skin is broken, cleanse it with a mild antiseptic (such as boric acid or peroxide) and apply boric acid ointment. If the hair falls out as a result of injury, rub Vaseline over the affected parts daily and massage gently. If the tail is broken, have it set.

SLEEPING PILLS AND TRANQUILIZERS

If you find your dog in the act of eating sleeping pills or tranquilizers, or if you have reason to believe he has just eaten them, empty his stomach immediately (as described under REMOVING FOREIGN OBJECTS FROM THE STOMACH), and give him some black coffee. If some time has elapsed and the pills have taken effect—if he sleeps too heavily and can't be awakened—massage him vigorously, flex his legs, wave ammonia or smelling salts under his nose, roll him around, try to stand him up and keep this action going constantly until you can get in touch with your veterinarian. The degree of your concern should, of course, depend upon how many he has eaten. I have known dogs who have eaten enough to knock them out for forty-eight hours or more and have come out unharmed.

All pills for humans should be kept well out of the range of dogs, as for some reason they love to eat pills; maybe it is because they are small and the dog believes they are designed especially for him, or thinks they are candy. In cautioning you to keep all pills out of the dog's range, I had better remind you that many dogs are highly talented, adept and dexterous and devious at ferreting out things they shouldn't ferret out, and pills are high on their list. I asked a woman recently how on earth her dog had got hold of a whole bottle of her own diuretic pills and she said he had opened her dresser drawer, taken them out and taken the top off the bottle. I believed her. I recently encountered the reverse of this common plight: A child ate the dog's pills. Her worried father called me in the middle of the night to find out what the pills were. They were sulfa pills—of small dosage fortunately, but still not a wholesome between-meals snack for a kiddie.

BATHROOM ACCIDENTS

While not as hazardous for dogs as it is (statistically) for human beings, the bathroom can also be the scene of accidents for dogs. A common practice of dog owners is to turn the hot water on in a tub for a bath for themselves, go about other business and, when they are ready for their baths, cool it down with cold water. A dog, particularly a young and frisky and incautious one, will take a flying leap and land right in a tub of scalding water. Or he will try to walk or stand on the edge of a tub and fall in. Wet tea bags and yellow oxide ointment are helpful home remedies for minor scalds, but a dog who has been scalded all over needs professional help and quickly.

Then there are owners who lock a dog in the bathroom when they go out. Left alone in a bathroom for a long period of time, more than one bored dog has turned on the water faucets, hot or cold; if he doesn't scald himself, he can flood the bathroom and the apartment below.

Because dogs use the toilet bowl as a drinking fountain, I have known several who got into trouble when detergents and lye-based powders were put into the bowls and were left there or were forgotten about.

CIGARETTE BURNS

Unless a burn is on the eye, it is not likely to be serious. If on the eye, put some strong tea on it, and follow later with a little castor oil or 1-per cent yellow oxide ointment. If the burn is bad and the dog persists in scratching it—and this goes for all persistent scratching of the head regions—put a Queen Elizabeth collar on him. A Queen Elizabeth collar (see illustration) is made of heavy cardboard or very light-weight wood. Cut a hole in the middle of it just big enough to fit around the dog's neck. Slit it down one side. Put it on the dog and then fasten the slit with adhesive tape. This will keep the dog from scratching his head. It will also make him unhappy. Dogs don't like to wear these collars, as a rule—not for reasons of discomfort particularly, but for reasons of pride. They think they look silly in them.

They seem to think they look silly in them.

CHAPTER FOURTEEN

The City Dog on Vacation

THE CITY DOG on vacation in the country leads a hazardous life. Ignorant of Nature and her weakness for practical jokes, foolhardy in the strictest city-slicker, wise-guy sense of the word, he gets fresh with snakes, porcupines and skunks and playful with beehives and hornets' nests. He eats poisonous garbage, gets covered with chiggers and ticks, catches his tail in a mole trap. He kills the neighbors' chickens and fights with their cats. At the seashore he eats sand, chokes on a fish bone or drowns. Under the spell of the full moon and the balmy nights, female city dogs forget all about the $10,000 champion stud they're engaged to and succumb to some rube far beneath them socially and twice their size.

Away from the safe and familiar lampposts and pavements, freed from the restraining influence of the leash, the city dog is a complete fool. And we must reckon with some of the pitfalls he is bound to fall into the moment he sets foot outside the city limits.

BEE OR HORNET STINGS

Apply a heavy paste of bicarbonate of soda or plain starch, or a solution of Zonite: one part Zonite to twenty parts water.

TICKS

See SKIN TROUBLES.

CHIGGERS

Chiggers are reddish mites, sometimes called grass mites, that burrow into the skins of dogs (and humans) and produce an itching which, if the dog scratches himself constantly, may result in sores.

Chiggers are hard to see with the naked eye. They attach to any part of the body, but they are easiest to see on the dog's abdomen. With the aid of a magnifying glass, you should be able to make an accurate diagnosis. The treatment is a Creolin bath as described in the chapter SKIN TROUBLES. Sulphur and lard is another treatment: one part sulphur to four parts lard. Still another good remedy is pyrethrum powder, and many of the commercial powders on the market are good. Any of these treatments will have to be repeated from time to time as new infestations appear. They are not preventives.

PORCUPINE QUILLS

Porcupine quills should be worked out, not yanked out. They should be slowly twisted and gradually loosened until the whole quill, down to its very tip, is dislodged and comes out intact. This is almost impossible to do and almost unbearably painful to the dog. Any dog with a good dose of porcupine quills in his hide should, rightfully, be completely anesthetized and have the quills taken out by a veterinarian. The next-best thing to do is to give the dog a sedative—half a grain or a grain of whatever barbiturate you have around, or a tranquilizer; repeat in half an hour and see if you can't get him calmed down a little. Or give him whisky, if you have no sedatives around. When he gets a bit groggy, try to work the quills out. After you've pulled each one out, put any standard antiseptic into the wounds as deeply as you can. If abscesses form later, it probably means that parts of the quills have been left under the skin. Removing embedded parts of porcupine quills constitutes a minor operation.

SNAKE BITES

Quick action is needed in dealing with bites from poisonous snakes. Make several incisions in and around the swelling and try to press the poison out as quickly as you can. Then put any kind of mild antiseptic into the openings—peroxide, iodine, diluted Zonite or straight whisky. If the bite is on the leg, put a tourniquet above it until you have finished treatment.

There are some excellent antivenom serums on the market for snake bites, and it would be a wise precaution for every dog owner to have some always on hand if he is going into snaky country.

SAND AND SALT-WATER TROUBLES

Until they've learned better, dogs will eat sand and drink salt water. They'll invariably vomit up salt water and usually they'll vomit up sand, but if they don't and get sick (vomiting, diarrhea, pains, etc.), give them repeated doses of mineral oil and a warm soap-and-water enema. Take them off their food for twenty-four hours, but give them plenty of water. Dogs with particularly tender skins often itch after salt water has dried in their coats, and they'll sometimes scratch themselves sore. Such dogs, until they get toughened up, should be given a fresh-water shower at night.

DROWNING

It's news when a human has to rescue a dog from drowning. Rescuing the drowning is the dog's specialty, and don't think he doesn't know it. There was a dog out on Long Island a few years ago who went rescue-crazy. A little boy was playing around in the fringes of the surf and got knocked down by a small wave. Before his parents could get to him to pick him up, the dog rushed in and rescued him. The boy's family and all the neighbors made a big fuss over the dog. They praised him; patted him; gave him extra food and cigars; let him sleep in the house, jump up on them, lie on the sofas. He had never had such attention in his life.

Unfortunately for all the other swimmers on the beach, success went to his head. Thereafter he tried to rescue everybody who went into the water and nearly succeeded in drowning a couple of good swimmers who foolishly tried to resist him. He got to be such a problem with his rescue work that the family finally had to tie him up every time they wanted to take a quiet swim.

Most dogs, of course, can swim. Put a two-month-old puppy in a bathtub and he thinks he's Johnny Weismuller. Occasionally, though, a dog will suffer cramps or exhaustion and have to be resuscitated. Resuscitation for dogs is about the same as one of the methods for man. Hold the dog up by his hind legs and let the water run out. Then press his ribs in and out slowly. If he is unconscious, try to revive him with aromatic spirits of ammonia held under his nose. If he is conscious give him whisky. Afterward wrap him in blankets and put hot-water bottles around him.

PREGNANCY

There's a section on this in the chapter on LOVE LIFE OF THE CITY DOG. It's the same—town or country.

FISHHOOKS

If the barbed end of the hook is exposed—if the hook has pierced right through a lip, say, or an ear lobe—cut off the barbed end with pliers, pull the straight part through and out, and treat with an antiseptic. If the barbed end is buried in the flesh and unexposed, don't pull on it and don't try to work it out. Get the dog to a veterinarian and have him cut it out. If the hook is in the tongue or in an eye, rush the dog to a veterinarian.

HEAT PROSTRATION

See FITS.

*Thunderstorms have driven more than one dog
into hysterics.*

HYSTERIA FROM THUNDERSTORMS
OR FROM FOURTH OF JULY CELEBRATIONS

This is quite common. Thunderstorms and Fourth of July celebrations have driven more than one dog into hysterics. Every Fourth of July without fail I have several urgent calls from vacationing owners whose dogs have gone into fits from the noise of firecrackers. If a dog is hysterical, give him a sedative—a barbiturate, a tranquilizer or Dramamine. And the same treatment goes for thunderstorms. I have seen many dogs apprehend thunderstorms an hour or two before they would actually break and crawl under a bed and shake all over. Pull the dog out from under the bed and give him a sedative; there is no point in allowing him to suffer.

GUNSHOT

Shot wounds seldom become infected, and sometimes it's wiser to leave the shot in the dog. If it is too near a vital spot, or if to remove it means cutting into an important muscle and thereby running the risk of crippling the dog, it is better to leave it in. The removal of shot or bullets is a job for a veterinarian. The dog must be fluoroscoped or X-rayed and the shot either removed or left, depending upon the veterinarian's findings and decision.

GARBAGE

The smell alone of some of the horrible objects a dog will ferret out of a garbage heap or dig up on a beach should by rights gas him. The most fastidious dogs and the ones most esthetically brought up will, when turned loose, act like scavengers. And sometimes they have to pay for their low tastes. Vomiting, cramps, fever, diarrhea, hives and sometimes convulsions are symptoms of food poisoning.

Induce vomiting by a teaspoonful or two of salt put on the

back of the dog's tongue. Give him an enema, as described under VOMITING. Then give him a dose of castor oil—a teaspoonful for small dogs, a tablespoonful for large dogs. Don't feed him for twenty-four hours afterward.

HOW TO STOP A DOGFIGHT

This is hard to do, and if the dogs are big it is dangerous for one person to try it singlehanded: the dogs may turn on him. Try pulling the dogs apart by their collars—one person to each dog—and have somebody else throw water on them. If the dogs are big and you are alone, you'd better stay out of the fray altogether. Cold water, however, will work most of the time. You may have to repeat the dousing a number of times.

RABIES

Rabies is chiefly a country-dog problem, not a city-dog problem, and for this reason I list it under THE CITY DOG ON VACATION. Rabies carries with it almost as many superstitions as a dream book. It is known as rabies ("to rave"), as hydrophobia ("fear of water") and as plain mad dog. It is one of the oldest diseases in the world, and its antiquity no doubt explains much of the misinformation and superstition that still cling to it. It has been passed down from the dark ages of superstitions, and though a great deal of light has been thrown upon the subject in the past century, it is still surrounded with many dark-ages fallacies, and the cry "Mad dog" can still cause hysteria in the most highly civilized communities. Some of the more common fallacies are that the disease is caused:

By hot weather.
By raw meat.
By lack of drinking water, or by polluted water or food.

("Fear of water" is not a canine symptom in rabies, but it often is in humans suffering from the disease.)
By sexual repression.
By a sudden drying up of milk in a nursing bitch.
By fright.

Another old belief is that a rabid person or animal, or one only exposed to a rabid person or animal, is able by his mere presence to infect other persons or whole communities. As late as the nineteenth century this belief still persisted, and large groups of suspects and victims were put to death in a wholesale manner. Smothering between mattresses or blankets was a common method used in disposing of the victims.

And there are, of course, the usual run of old beliefs, still occasionally to be found, that the disease is caused by certain stars, by periods of the moon or by evil spirits.

METHOD OF TRANSMISSION

Rabies is found in animals, birds and fowl in the wild state, which is the reason for discussion in this chapter. Few dogs in their city homes run into foxes, bats or raccoons. Rabies belongs to the group of virus diseases. The virus is present in the saliva of the dog and the usual method of transmission is through a bite wound. Infection is possible also if the saliva comes into contact with already broken skin. Infection is not possible if the virus enters the mouth unless there are lesions present in the mouth or throat. These are the only ways in which rabies can be contracted.

SYMPTOMS OF THE DISEASE

A disease of the nervous system, rabies occurs in two forms, the furious and the dumb.

There are, as a rule, three stages in the furious type of rabies: the melancholic, the excited and the paralytic, though there is seldom a recognizable dividing line between the succeeding stages; they blend and overlap, and the symptoms vary, so that it is hard to say this is stage one, this stage three, etc. Nevertheless, I will describe the three stages as they appear most often:

The first symptom is usually dullness and gloominess, and the dog has a tendency to hide. Or he may become pitiably affectionate as if seeking comfort. Restlessness is common. The dog will crawl disconsolately under a table and hide only to become suddenly alert and active. Sometimes there is a disposition to lick such things as floors, furniture, windows and hearths and to swallow unusual objects like pieces of paper, bits of wood or string. The dog is often nervous and easily startled by noises or movements or sudden light; sometimes sexual excitability is noticed. This stage lasts usually from one to three days.

In the excited stage, the dog becomes vicious and has a tendency to tear things up if he is confined. If he isn't confined he will probably wander away from home, biting other dogs or persons who happen to cross his path. His whole facial expression changes, and he has a definite mad look in his eyes. Barking increases in this stage. The barking is characterized by hoarseness, which is due to oncoming paralysis. This stage lasts usually from two to four days.

The paralytic stage begins with the tongue, jaw and throat. The dog experiences loss of voice, inability to swallow, inability to close his mouth and drooling of saliva. The hind legs are usually affected next, and complete paralysis follows. The dog dies in a coma within twenty-four hours.

The dog suffering from dumb rabies may have one or all of the early symptoms of furious rabies, but most generally paralysis of the lower jaw and tongue is the first noticeable and, throughout the course of the disease, most prominent symptom. The lower jaw hangs down and the tongue out, making swallowing and barking impossible. The dog shows a peculiar haunted look in his eyes and other dispirited symptoms and, in the majority of cases, no signs of viciousness or attempts to bite. As the name "dumb" implies, it is a quiet disease—a spreading of the paralytic symptoms from the throat and tongue to all parts of the body. Death occurs usually within five to seven days.

TREATMENT FOR RABIES BITES

If a human has been bitten, a physician should be consulted at once for proper antirabic treatment.

If another dog is bitten, the wound should be opened immediately in several places and any strong antiseptic available applied heavily to the wound until a veterinarian can be found and antirabic treatment administered. Antirabic treatments today are just about perfect in results.

PREVENTIVE INOCULATIONS

Like the antirabic treatments, the preventive inoculations have been developed and almost perfected during the past few years. They are not as yet permanently protective—they have to be repeated—but they are almost a hundred per cent reliable. Have your dog inoculated before you take him to the country. Or if he has been previously inoculated, ask your veterinarian about inoculating him again.

TRAVEL PROBLEMS

If you plan to take a trip with a dog anywhere at all—except to the corner grocery—the first thing to do is get from your veterinarian: (1) a health certificate with statements on it of inoculations for distemper, infectious hepatitis and leptospirosis and (2) a rabies certificate with a rabies tag to put on the dog's collar.

Some states in this country have stringent health laws about dogs; some don't. Some airlines want health certificates; some don't. Some railroads do; some don't. Because most dogs have had all of these inoculations anyhow (starting with puppyhood), and because it is so easy to get the certificates, and because you just might be asked for one or more of them by some zealous guardian of the law while crossing some state line by car, or at an airport or railroad station, you should get them and keep them right along with your traveler's checks and the keys to your luggage.

This way you will be prepared for any questioning that might come up, which could lead to heated arguments, and worse, as a boxer patient of mine found out the hard way. He and his owner have driven across the country at least a dozen times and they have never been stopped or questioned—but once. Though the dog was wearing his rabies tag, the Law, on this occasion, wanted to see his rabies certificate and health certificate. The owner didn't have them. This led to explanations, to claims, to the raising of voices, and the dog, taking his owner's side in the argument, tried to bite the officer. Their trip was held up at that juncture for four days.

If you plan to travel abroad, take your whole set of certificates with you. Again, some countries will want only a rabies certificate or a health certificate, but others may prove very nosy about other aspects of your dog's health. (So far, no certificate of mental health is needed, but that will probably come some day.) And be sure to check on the quarantine regulations of the country or countries you plan to visit. Great Britain, Finland, Denmark, Sweden, Ireland and Hawaii I know have periods of quarantine, and other countries are following suit (Russia doesn't allow dogs in at all), so find out from your travel agent or from the consulate what the laws are where you are going, or you and your dog might find yourselves sitting on the front steps of some country, not allowed in.

A dog can travel with his owner on most trains if the owner buys enclosed space (drawing room, bedroom); otherwise he must travel in the baggage car. He can travel on a port-to-port basis on most ships—in the ship's kennels or, on some ships, in the owner's stateroom. On most planes the dog must be crated and put in the belly of the plane. On some transatlantic flights, one dog per flight is allowed in the cabin with his owner, a tricky ruling if I ever heard one. For the privilege of being that one and only dog I should think reservations would have to be made far ahead of time (and checked every day or two to see if the ruling still held). Dogs are not allowed on cruise ships or on the major cross-country buses.

As for shipping by rail or air, call the lines about their regulations. Some furnish their own crates for your use. Some want you to furnish them. There are rules about feeding, about health certificates, about muzzles and about a lot of other things, all varying. There are kennels that will take on the job of crating and shipping for you, so call up some kennels in your locality and you will probably be able to locate such a service.

I have never taken a major trip with a dog, but I have been told over the years by many scores of globe-trotting owners that dogs are excellent travelers. At one time I would have thought the opposite; I would have thought the unfamiliar would make them nervous; but the glowing reports of all of those returning travelers and the glowing conditions of the dogs themselves have changed my mind.

Dogs are often better travelers than people. I know a nervous, jumpy man, an apprehensive traveler, who takes his dog with him on all of his vacation trips because the dog is so poised and calm that he calms the owner down. He is particularly solacing and soothing on board ship, the owner claims, when he himself is feeling queasy; the dog holds his hand.

Dogs are also enthusiastic travelers, I am told; new sights and scents are interesting and exciting to them. I know another dog owner who takes her dog with her on trips because, she says, she finds his joyousness infectious. (I know people who travel with people, too, but their testimonials are not, for some reason, quite as laudatory as the ones for the canine companions.)

Though in the minority, there are poor travelers in the dog set. Car, train, sea and air sickness are fairly common among them and, occasionally, hysteria. If you have one of these unfortunates, don't feed him for several hours before a trip and don't give him any water. Give him a little Dramamine an hour ahead of time, or a tranquilizer, and on long trips repeat the dose if necessary.

I would take these precautions always on a first trip with a dog. He will probably turn out to be calm, poised and joyous, but I would want to play it safe on that first trip to see just what his potential is for globe-trotting. Even seasoned travelers (dogs and humans) are frequently beset by that bane to travelers, diarrhea. Paregoric is a good item to take on a trip, and Kaopectate can be bought almost anywhere; they are both standard stand-bys. And take the dog off food and water for twenty-four hours.

The Gaines Dog Research Center, 250 Park Avenue, New York, New York 10017, has a file of hotels and motels from Maine to California that will allow dogs, and you can get this file by writing to the center and enclosing twenty-five cents. It is called "Touring with Towser." If you don't want to tour with Towser—if you want to board him out while you are away—the Gaines people will accommodate you with another booklet called "Where to Buy, Board or Train a Dog," which contains a national list of investigated boarding houses. This booklet is free.

European hotels and motels, I am told, are more widely hospitable to dogs than we are, but I don't know of any overall guide to such hostelries. In France, the Michelin guide is specific about where dogs are or are not welcomed. For travel outside of France, you will have to take this problem up with somebody else, such as the consulates of the countries you plan to visit. As an international guide I am afraid I have shot my bolt.

CHAPTER FIFTEEN

Menus

Up until two months the puppy will be nursing and/or on a milk formula with occasional beef scrapings if he likes them. (See CARE OF PUPPIES.) I would let him and his mother be the judges of how much and how often he wants to nurse or eat during that period.

DIETS FOR TOY BREEDS

(Dogs such as Chihuahuas, papillons, Pomeranians, black-and-tan terriers, Japanese spaniels, Brussels griffons, English toy spaniels, toy Manchester terriers, Yorkshire terriers, Shih Tzus, Malteses, silky terriers, Italian greyhounds)

TWO MONTHS

Morning	Two or three tablespoonfuls milk formula*
Late morning	Two heaping teaspoonfuls chopped beef. (Substitute lamb, mutton or fish occasionally.†)

* Milk formula: one pint milk, one tablespoonful limewater, one tablespoonful sugar of milk or corn syrup or honey, one whole egg.
† Keep these substitutes in mind, because the menus mention beef only.

Early afternoon	Two or three tablespoonfuls milk formula.
Evening	One heaping tablespoonful chopped beef, one teaspoonful puréed vegetables, one slice of toast.
Late evening	Two to three tablespoonfuls milk formula. One-half teaspoonful cod-liver oil daily.

THREE MONTHS

Morning	Two or three tablespoonfuls milk formula.
Late morning	One heaping tablespoonful chopped beef.
Early afternoon	Two to three tablespoonfuls milk formula.
Evening	Two heaping tablespoonfuls chopped beef, one piece of toast, two teaspoonfuls puréed or well-cooked vegetables.
Late evening	Two to three tablespoonfuls milk formula. One-half teaspoonful cod-liver oil twice a day.

FOUR MONTHS

Morning	Four to six tablespoonfuls milk formula.
Noon	Two heaping tablespoonfuls chopped beef.
Evening	Two to three heaping tablespoonfuls chopped beef, two to three teaspoonfuls vegetables, a slice of toast.
Late evening	Four to six tablespoonfuls milk formula. One teaspoonful cod-liver oil daily.

FIVE MONTHS

Morning	Four to six tablespoonfuls milk formula.
Noon	Two heaping tablespoonfuls chopped beef.
Evening	Three heaping tablespoonfuls chopped beef, three teaspoonfuls vegetables, a piece of toast.
Late evening	Four to six tablespoonfuls milk formula. One teaspoonful cod-liver oil twice a day.

SIX MONTHS

Morning   Four to six tablespoonfuls milk.
An egg three or four times a week.
Noon   Two heaping tablespoonfuls chopped beef.
Evening   Three heaping tablespoonfuls chopped beef, one tablespoonful vegetables, a piece of toast.
One teaspoonful cod-liver oil twice a day.

SEVEN, EIGHT, NINE AND TEN MONTHS

(Gradually increasing amounts until eleventh month)

Morning   Three-fourths cup milk with a raw egg.
Noon   Two heaping tablespoonfuls chopped beef.
Evening   Three to four heaping tablespoonfuls chopped beef, three to four tablespoonfuls vegetables, a piece of toast.
One teaspoonful cod-liver oil twice a day.

ELEVEN TO TWELVE MONTHS

Morning   Two heaping tablespoonfuls chopped beef and a slice of toast.
An egg two or three times a week.
Evening   Four heaping tablespoonfuls chopped beef, one tablespoonful vegetables, a piece of toast.
One teaspoonful cod-liver oil twice a day.

THIRTEEN MONTHS AND UP

Same feedings as for eleven and twelve months, unless the dog seems to require more or less food.
Cod-liver oil is usually discontinued after a year.

Diets for Small Breeds

(Dogs such as wire-haired terriers, cocker spaniels, cairn terriers, dachshunds, beagles, West Highland terriers, Scotties, Sealyhams, Australian terriers, Lhasa apsos, corgis, Skye terriers, small French poodles, large Pekingeses, Welsh terriers, Dandie Dinmonts, whippets, Irish terriers, Bedlington terriers, French bulls, small schnauzers, pugs)

TWO MONTHS

Morning	Three to four tablespoonfuls milk formula and a piece of toast.
Noon	Two heaping tablespoonfuls chopped beef.
Evening	Two heaping tablespoonfuls chopped beef, a slice of toast, one tablespoonful cooked vegetables.
Late evening	Three tablespoonfuls milk formula. One teaspoonful cod-liver oil daily.

THREE MONTHS

Morning	Four tablespoonfuls milk formula and a piece of toast.
Noon	Two heaping tablespoonfuls chopped beef with a slice of toast.
Evening	Three heaping tablespoonfuls chopped beef, a slice of toast, a tablespoonful cooked vegetables.
Late evening	Four tablespoonfuls milk formula. One teaspoonful cod-liver oil twice a day.

FOUR MONTHS

Morning	Six to eight tablespoonfuls milk formula with a piece of toast.
Noon	Three heaping tablespoonfuls chopped beef with a slice of toast.

Evening	Four heaping tablespoonfuls chopped beef, a slice of toast, two tablespoonfuls vegetables.
Late evening	One cup milk formula.
	One teaspoonful cod-liver oil twice a day.

FIVE MONTHS

Morning	Six to eight tablespoonfuls milk formula with a slice of toast.
Noon	Three heaping tablespoonfuls chopped beef with a slice of toast.
Evening	Four to five heaping tablespoonfuls chopped beef, two tablespoonfuls vegetables.
Late evening	One cup milk formula.
	Two teaspoonfuls cod-liver oil twice a day.

SIX MONTHS

Morning	One cup milk and two pieces of toast.
	An egg four or five times a week.
Noon	Three to four heaping tablespoonfuls chopped beef and a slice of toast.
Evening	Five to six heaping tablespoonfuls chopped beef, two tablespoonfuls cooked vegetables, two pieces of toast.
	Two teaspoonfuls cod-liver oil twice a day.

SEVEN, EIGHT, NINE AND TEN MONTHS

(Gradually increasing amounts from seven months on)

Morning	One cup milk and two pieces of toast.
	An egg four or five times a week.
Noon	Four heaping tablespoonfuls chopped beef and a slice of toast.
Evening	Six to eight tablespoonfuls chopped beef, two tablespoonfuls cooked vegetables, two pieces of toast.

175

ELEVEN AND TWELVE MONTHS

Morning	One cup milk and two pieces of toast.
	An egg four or five times a week.
Evening	One-half to three-quarters of a pound chopped beef, two tablespoonfuls cooked vegetables, two pieces of toast.
	One teaspoonful cod-liver oil daily.

THIRTEEN MONTHS AND UP

Same as for eleven and twelve months with slight reduction or increase in portions if required. Cod-liver oil is usually discontinued after a year.

DIETS FOR LARGE BREEDS

(Dogs such as Airedales, Dalmations, Irish setters, Samoyeds, pointers, English and Gordon setters, schnauzers, Doberman pinschers, greyhounds, Kerry blues, large spaniels, shepherds, collies, large French poodles, salukis, chows, Afghans, Labrador and Chesapeake Bay retrievers, Briards, bulldogs, basset hounds, old English sheep dogs, otterhounds, clumber spaniels, Irish terriers, Bouviers des Flandres, Weimaraners, German short-haired pointers)

TWO MONTHS

Morning	One cup milk formula and a piece of toast.
Noon	Three heaping tablespoonfuls chopped beef.
Afternoon	One cup milk formula.
Evening	Three to four heaping tablespoonfuls chopped beef, one tablespoonful vegetables, two slices of toast.
Late evening	One cup milk formula.
	One teaspoonful cod-liver oil twice a day.

176

THREE MONTHS

Morning	One glass milk formula and two pieces of toast.
Noon	Three to four heaping tablespoonfuls chopped beef.
Evening	Four heaping tablespoonfuls chopped beef, two tablespoonfuls cooked vegetables, two slices of toast.
Late evening	One glass milk formula.
	One teaspoonful cod-liver oil twice a day.

FOUR MONTHS

Morning	One glass milk formula with two pieces of toast.
Noon	Four heaping tablespoonfuls chopped beef.
Evening	Six heaping tablespoonfuls chopped beef, one cup of vegetables, two slices of toast.
Late evening	One glass milk formula.
	Two teaspoonfuls cod-liver oil twice a day.

FIVE MONTHS

Morning	One glass milk formula and two pieces of toast.
Noon	Four to five tablespoonfuls chopped beef.
Evening	Eight tablespoonfuls chopped beef, one cup vegetables, two slices of toast.
Late evening	One glass milk formula.
	Two to three teaspoonfuls cod-liver oil twice a day.

SIX MONTHS

Morning	One pint milk and a raw egg. Three pieces of toast.
Noon	One-half pound chopped beef.

Evening
: One-half pound chopped beef, one cup vegetables.
One tablespoonful cod-liver oil twice a day.

SEVEN, EIGHT, NINE AND TEN MONTHS

Morning
: One pint milk, one raw egg, three or four pieces of toast.

Noon
: One-half pound chopped beef.

Evening
: Three-quarters of a pound to one pound chopped beef, one cup vegetables, two or three pieces of stale bread.
One tablespoonful cod-liver oil twice a day.

ELEVEN AND TWELVE MONTHS

Morning
: One pint milk, one raw egg, three or four pieces of toast.

Evening
: One to one and a half pounds chopped beef, one or two cups cooked vegetables, four or five pieces of toast or stale bread.

THIRTEEN MONTHS AND UP

Same as for eleven and twelve months, with slight increase or reduction in portions if required.
Cod-liver oil is usually discontinued after a year.

DIETS FOR VERY LARGE BREEDS

(Dogs such as great Danes, Newfoundlands, bloodhounds, Irish wolfhounds, Russian wolfhounds, St. Bernards, mastiffs, Rottweilers, Italian bulls, great Pyrenees)

TWO MONTHS

Morning
: Two cups milk formula.

178

Noon	One-quarter pound chopped beef and two or three pieces of toast.
Evening	One-half pound chopped beef, one cup cooked vegetables, two pieces of toast.
Late evening	Two cups milk formula.
	One tablespoonful cod-liver oil once a day.

THREE MONTHS

Morning	One pint milk formula, one raw egg, three or four pieces of toast.
Noon	One-half pound chopped beef and four slices of toast or stale bread.
Evening	Three-quarters of a pound chopped beef, two cups vegetables, two pieces of toast or stale bread.
Late evening	One pint of milk formula.
	One tablespoonful cod-liver oil twice a day.

FOUR MONTHS

Morning	One pint milk formula, one raw egg, three or four pieces of toast.
Noon	Three-quarters of a pound to one pound chopped beef.
Evening	One pound chopped beef, two cups vegetables, two pieces of toast or stale bread.
	One tablespoonful cod-liver oil twice a day.

FIVE MONTHS

Morning	One pint milk formula, one raw egg, four or five pieces of toast.
Noon	One to one and a half pounds chopped beef.
Evening	One to one and a half pounds chopped beef, two or three cups cooked vegetables, three pieces of toast or stale bread.
Late evening	One pint milk formula.

One and a half tablespoonfuls cod-liver oil twice a day.

SIX MONTHS

Morning	One and a half pints milk, two eggs, four or five pieces of toast.
Noon	One and a half pounds chopped beef.
Evening	One and a half to two pounds chopped beef, three or four cups vegetables, four or five pieces of toast. One and a half to two tablespoonfuls cod-liver oil twice a day.

SEVEN, EIGHT, NINE AND TEN MONTHS

Morning	One quart milk, two eggs, four or five pieces of toast.
Noon	Two pounds chopped beef.
Evening	Two to three pounds chopped beef, three or four cups vegetables, four or five pieces stale whole-wheat bread. One and a half to two tablespoonfuls cod-liver oil twice a day.

ELEVEN AND TWELVE MONTHS

Morning	One quart milk, two eggs, three or four pieces of toast or stale bread.
Evening	Three to three and a half pounds chopped beef, three or four cups cooked vegetables, half a dozen pieces of stale whole-wheat bread.

Index

Abortion, 98
Accidents, 150–157
Affection, 57–58
Afterbirth, 101
Air sickness, 170
Airedale, 81
Alcohol
  in cleaning, 77
  in diet, 48–49
  medicinal use of, 99, 108,
    109, 153, 159, 160, 161
American Kennel Club, 23–24,
  25, 31, 68, 69
Ammonia, 160
Anal abscesses, 144–145
Antibiotics, 125, 138
Antihistamines, 108
Appetite, 47
Argyrol, 126, 136
Asthma, 142
Aureomycin, 126

Balsam of Peru, 108, 110

Barking, 66–67, 83
Baskets, 100
Bathing, 72, 75–77, 104–105,
  108, 110
Bathroom accidents, 156
Bay rum, 77
Beagle, 30–31
Bedding, 106, 110
Bee stings, 158
Beef, 102, 128
Begging, 68
Bicarbonate of soda, 102, 108,
  126, 140, 147, 158
Birth. *See* Whelping
Bismuth formic iodide powder,
  145
Bitches
  breeding, 97
  celibacy, 93–96
  contraception, 97, 98
  diseases, reproductive, 147–
    149
  false pregnancy, 103
  lactation, 102

Bitches (*continued*)
  vs. males, as pets, 28–30
  mating, 98–99
  menstruation, 95, 103
  pregnancy, 99
  spaying, 92–103
  sterilization, 96–97
  whelping, 100–102
Biting, 82–83, 167
Bladder stones, 143, 144
Blindness, 133
Blue eye, 135–136
Bluetick hounds, 31
Bone development, 146
Bones, 46
Boric acid, 108, 126, 136, 138,
    145, 153 154
Boston terriers, 145
Breasts, 99, 102
Breeding, 33–35, 97–98
Brushing, 72, 74
Buckthorn, syrup of, 113
Bulldogs, 142
Burns, 156–157

Caecum, 117
Calcium gluconate, 108
Calcium lactate, 142, 146
Camphorated oil, 102, 127, 138
Cancer, 149
Car sickness, 170
Cascara sagrada, 141
Castor oil, 76, 99, 113
Castration, 92–96, 109
Cataracts, 137
Celibacy, 93–96
Charcoal tablets, 147

Chewing gum, 75
Chiggers, 159
Children, and dogs, 34–36
Chill, 143
Chloromycetin, 126
Chorea (St. Vitus' dance), 133
Cigarette burns, 156–157
Clipping, 74
Clothing, 86–89
Coat. *See* Hair
Coats, 72, 88, 146
Coccidiosis, 118
Coconut oil, 107
Cod-liver oil, 48, 128, 146
Colds, 86
Collars, 89
  flea collar, 105
  to prevent scratching, 108,
    110, 157
Color blindness, 56
Columbia University, 29, 51
Combing, 72, 106
Companionship, between dogs,
  38–40
Congestion, 127
Conjunctivitis, 137
Constipation, 99, 139, 140, 141,
  147
Contagion, 110. *See also*
  Quarantine
Contraception, 97, 98
Convulsions. *See* Fits
Cornell University, 29
Coughing, 133, 142, 149
Cramps, 160
Creolin, 104, 105, 108, 110, 159
Curb training, 63–64
Cuts, 153–154
Cystitis, 143

Dandruff, 107
Depression, 131–132
Derris bath, 77, 104
Diarrhea, 127, 140
Diets, 171–180. *See also*
  Feeding
Diseases, 18, 80. *See also*
  specific diseases
Distemper, 80, 123–133, 136,
  139, 140, 147
Doberman pinschers, 37–38
Dog fights, 164
Dognaping, 89
Douching, 98, 101, 148
Dramamine, 170
Dreams, erotic, 96
Drowning, 160–161
Dry cleaning, 77
Durham-Enders Razor Corpo-
  ration, 71

Ear clipping, 70
Ear shortening, 70
Ears, 75, 138–139
Eczema, 107–109
Egg whites, 154
Electric shocks, 153
Elevators, 86
Ellin Prince Speyer Hospital,
  16, 47
Enemas, 122, 140, 141
English bulls, 136
Escalators, 86
Ether, 75
Eucalyptus oil, 127
Exercise, 41
Eyelids, 136
Eyes, 135–136, 137, 146

Eyesight, 56, 86

Falls, 156
False pregnancy, 102
Fat, 48
Fatigue, 54–55
Feeding, 42–50
Feet, 86, 88
Females. *See* Bitches
Fever, 26, 125, 134
Field trainers, 56
Fighting, 84
Filariae, 114, 115, 117
Fishhooks, 161–162
Fistula, dental, 147
Fits, 119–122, 127, 143
Flea collar, 105
Fleas, 77, 104–105
Follicular mange. *See* Mange
Foods, 48
Force-feeding, 130
Foreign objects, 151–152

Gaines Dog Research Center,
  170
Galoshes, 86
Garlic, 118
Genital disorders, 143
Georgia redbone hound, 31
German shepherd, 30, 34, 37,
  51–52
Gloving, 72
Glycerine, 99, 139, 141, 142
Great Danes, 136
Green soap, tincture of, 77
Grooming, 70–90
Gunshot wounds, 163

Hair, 72, 107, 110
Halitosis, 147
Harder's gland, inflamed, 13
Harelips, 71
Harnesses, 88–89
Health certificates, 167–168
Hearing, 56, 81
Heartworm. *See Filariae*
Heat, 95
Heat hysteria, 122
Heeling, 64–65
Hemorrhage, 153
Hemorrhoids. *See* Anal
    abscesses
Hepatitis, 80, 126, 136, 139
Hip dysplasia, 145
Hookworm, 114, 117
Hormones, 102, 149
Hornet stings, 158
Horses, 84
Hospitals, 132
Housebreaking, 56, 57, 61–64
Hysteria, 163

Ice packs, 122
Immunization, 135
Incontinence, 127, 133
Infectious hepatitis, 134
Inhalants, 142
Inoculations, 124, 169
Insecticides, 106, 139
Iodine, 109, 160
Itching, 110

Jealousy, 35, 39–40
Johns Hopkins Hospital, 29, 53, 54

Jumping, 65–66

Kaopectate, 140, 170
Kerosene, 75, 107
Kerosene-and-milk bath, 104, 105
Kidney disorder, 139
Kidney stones, 143

Laxatives, 141–142, 144
Leash training, 64–65, 84, 86
Leptospirosis, 18, 80, 135
Lessons, 54–55
Lice, 105–106
Lip shortening, 70
Listlessness, 146
Loya, Alfred, 56
Lumps, 149

Males
    breeding, 98
    castration, 92–93
    celibacy, 93–96
    curb training, 64
    diseases, reproductive, 147–149
    vs. females, as pets, 28–30
    mating, 98–99
Mange, 109–111
    in humans, 18
Manners. *See* Training
Massages, 77–79
Mating, 98–99
Meals. *See* Diets, Feeding
Meat, 46
Memory, 54

Meningitis, 135
Menstruation, 103
Menus, 171–180
Mercuric oxide ointment, 126, 138, 139
Milk, 46, 102
Milk of magnesia, 108, 140, 141
Mineral oil, 99, 126, 141, 152, 160
Mineral tablets, 49
Miscarriage, 99
Mites, 139, 159
Mongrels, 31–32
Mustard water, 151
Muzzles, 83

Nervous breakdown, 53–54
Nervousness, 66
New York City law, 83
Nipples, 102
Nits, 106
Noerr, Robert, 69
Noses, 126
Nupercainal ointment, 138
Nursing, 102

Obedience classes, 68–69
Obesity, 142, 143
Oiling, 72
Oils, 48. *See also* specific oils
Olive oil, 75, 138, 139
Overfeeding, 44

Pads, foot, 86, 88
Paint poisoning, 154

Paralysis, 133, 146–147
Parasites, 84
Paregoric, 140, 170
Pavlovian Laboratories, 53, 54
Paws. *See* Pads, foot
Pedicuring, 74–75
Penicillin, 126
Penis, 148–149
Peroxide, 75, 138, 153, 160
Perspiration, 72
Pet shops, 24–25
Plastic surgery, 70
Plucking, 74
Poisoning, 139–140
    arsenic, 154
    food, 163–164
    paint, 154
    snake, 160
    strychnine, 154
Pomeranians, 142
Poodle, 30, 71
Porcupine quills, 159
Potassium permanganate, 148, 149
Pregnancy, 99. *See also* False pregnancy
Prepared foods, 49–50
Prolapsed rectum, 145
Punishment, 52, 58–60
Puppies
    accidents, 150, 151, 153
    care of newborn, 102
    choice of, 21–26
    cleaning, 77
    coccidiosis, 118
    diarrhea, 127
    distemper, 124
    feeding, 44, 47, 171
    in hot weather, 122

Puppies (*continued*)
  housebreaking, 61–63
  inoculations, 134
  rickets, 146
  teething, 142–143
  training, 56–57, 80
  worming, 113–114, 116
Puppy worms. *See* Round-
  worms
Pyrethrum powder, 159
Pyribenzamine, 108

Quarantine regulations, in
  foreign countries, 168
Queen Elizabeth collar, 108,
  110, 157

Rabies, 19, 83, 164–167
Rectal syringe, 140
Rectum, prolapsed, 145
Registration, 25
Reproductive organs, diseases
  of, 147
Reward, 52
Rickets, 145
Ringling Brothers Circus, 56
Ringworm, 18, 109
Rotenone, 77, 104
Roundworms, 113–114, 116
Rubber gloves, 109, 110

St. Bernards, 136
St. Vitus' dance, 133
Salicylic acid, 108, 145
Salt water, 160

Saltpeter, 94–95
Sand, 160
Sarcoptic mange. *See* Mange
Scabs, 108
Scalding, 156
Scraps, 47
Scratching, 108
Screw-tail irritations, 145
Seasickness, 170
Sedatives. *See* Tranquilizers
Seeing Eye dogs, 56
Seeing Eye Institute for the
  Blind, 34
Sex, 28–29
Shampooing. *See* Bathing
Shock, 122
Showing, 69
Sight hounds, 56
Skin grafting, 70
Skin problems, 77, 104–111
Smell, 56
Snake bites, 160
Sores, 108
Spaying. *See* Castration
Speyer Hospital. *See* Ellin
  Prince Speyer Hospital
Sponging, 74
Starch, 158
Sterilization, 96–97
Sties, 136
Stings, 158
Stomach, 145, 150–152
Strychnine, 141, 142
Studs, 95, 98
Sulfa drugs, 118, 138
Sulphur, 46–47, 159
Suppositories, 99
Sweaters, 88
Swimming, 160–161

Tail bobbing, 70
Tail injury, 155
Tannic acid, 108, 145
Tapeworm, 114, 115
Tartar, 143, 147
Tattooing, 89–90
Tea, 153, 156
Teeth, 126, 147
Teething, 142–143
Terramycin, 126
Testicles, 148–149
Thermometer, 125
Ticks, 77, 106–107
Tourniquet, 154
Toxicity, 143
Training, 51–69
Tranquilizers, 67, 109, 120, 153,
    155–156, 159, 163, 170
Traveling, 158–170
Tricks, 67–68
Tuberculosis, 149
Turpentine, 75

Ulcers, 126
Underweight, 44
Urethral stones, 143
Urination, 148
Urine
   blood in, 148, 152
   retention, 143–144
Urotropin, 143, 144

Vacations. See Traveling
Vaseline, 145, 155
Viosterol, 48
Vitamins, 49, 108, 128, 146
Vomiting, 139–140, 152, 153,
    163–164
Vulva, 148

Walking, 80–90
Wardrobe, 86, 88
Watchdogs, 36–38
Weaning, 102
Westminster Kennel Club
   Show, 69
Wheezing, 142
Whelping, 100–102
Whipping. See Punishment
Whipworm, 114, 116–117
Worms, 18, 44, 112–122, 140
Wormseed, 113

X-ray treatment, 109, 115

Yellow oxide ointment, 156

Zonite, 158, 160

A Note About the Author

Dr. James R. Kinney *is a graduate of the University of Pennsylvania School of Veterinary Medicine. He has been practicing for over forty years, thirty-one of them at the Ellin Prince Speyer Hospital in New York City, where he was for 25 years Chief Veterinarian and Director. He is also Chief Veterinarian of the most important and biggest indoor dog show in the United States—the Westminster Kennel Club Show at Madison Square Garden in New York City.*

In all his years of practice he has been bitten by dogs only twice, and on both occasions he says it was his fault and not the dog's.

All dogs to him are "he" and all cats "she." Horses and other animals, and all birds, are "it," with the exception of canaries. Whether a bass or a coloratura, a canary is always "she."

Dr. Kinney is now in private practice and considers he lives a useful, full and rewarding life. His publisher's estimate would be that more than half the dogs in New York City concur.